THE JOY *of* SERVING GOD

THE JOY

of

SERVING GOD

by

DOM BASIL HEMPHILL, O.S.B.

B. HERDER BOOK CO.

15 & 17 SOUTH BROADWAY, ST. LOUIS 2, MO.

AND

33 QUEEN SQUARE, LONDON, W. C.

Library of Congress Catalog Card Number: 48-10168

IMPRIMI POTEST

H. K. Byrne, O.S.B.,

Abb. Pres.

Hereford, 25th May 1948

NIHIL OBSTAT

Innocentius Swoboda, O.F.M.,

Censor Librorum

IMPRIMATUR

✠ Joseph E. Ritter

Archiepiscopus

St. Ludovici, die 22 Junii, 1948

To

THE SISTERS OF MERCY

of Clifford, Yorks

THIS BOOK IS DEDICATED

IN GRATITUDE AND ADMIRATION

PREFACE

The conferences that follow are addressed primarily to those who are consecrated to God in the religious life, but to a great extent all Christians may apply to themselves much of what is said in them, especially the general theme of the book: the joy that characterizes the truths of our religion, and that should pervade our practice of it. For joy is of great value in our life and a powerful help to us in running our course, since it sweetens and makes all things easy. And this is especially true of community life, with its own peculiar burdens and difficulties arising from its unending routine and the inevitable frictions and irritations so apt to arise when people of varying temperaments, upbringing, and tastes have to live together in one house throughout their lives. In such circumstances a joyful outlook makes all the difference: it is the best antidote to, and preservative against, discouragement, weariness, and petty annoyances of all sorts, while at the same time it is a powerful help toward holiness. A holy religious is, contrary to the popular notion, a cheerful soul; and founders of religious orders have always inculcated cheerfulness in their followers. The opposite is equally true: that sadness and melancholy are bad signs in a religious and that the devil tries to make us gloomy, since innumerable ills and dangers follow from such a state.

Joy, then, should characterize the religious.[1] Joy, as Scripture and the Fathers teach, is the fruit of charity. This fact explains much and also indicates how to acquire the spirit of joy. Because joy springs from love of God, the life of a good religious is necessarily joyful, for the religious life is essentially a "love affair" with God. Unless love is at the root of it, dominating it, our religious life is but outward show and formalism, lacking in its most essential quality. But since it is the service of Him whom we love, it is necessarily joyful. That is one reason—there are others—why an observant and fervent community is always a happy one; whereas the laxer a house is the more discontented its members are. Observance and fervor spring from love of God; the more love, the more joy.

Thus religion and joy are bound up together, and it is highly significant that, whereas this has always been exemplified by Catholicism, the various heresies have been for the most part gloomy and forbidding. It was so in the early ages in the case of the Manichaeans, and later on with the Albigensians; in more modern times there have been the rigid sternness of Jansenism, the appalling melancholy and pessimism of Calvinism and Lutheranism, and the bleak cheerlessness of Presbyterianism with its characteristically unhappy Sabbatarianism. But Catholicism

---

[1] "We would greatly deceive ourselves if we thought that a sacrifice is of value and pleasing to God only when it is sorrowful and a mortification of nature. Scripture shows that God accepts sacrifices of flowers and fruit as well as those of blood, and sacrifices that are joyful as well as those that are offered with tears." Msgr. Gay.

has always been cheerful—hence the "Merrie England" of pre-Reformation days—and this joy manifests itself, especially in thoroughly Catholic lands, in the simple and childlike joy with which the great festivals of the Church and holydays of obligation are kept.[2]

And if joy should mark out the Christian (and truly he has innumerable causes for joy), this is especially true of the religious, for he or she has received in addition the happiness of a vocation to serve God in special intimacy. The grace of vocation to the religious life is bestowed by God in His inscrutable wisdom on those to whom He pleases to give it, and it is an inestimable privilege. How great a privilege we do not perhaps always realize. "If thou didst but know the gift of God" (John 4:10). If we could fully appreciate this wonderful gift, what a difference it would make to us, and how it would fill us with abiding and unshakable joy!

The chapters that go to make up this book were not devised to illustrate the title of the volume; in fact, the dominating idea of joy was not in the author's mind at all while composing them; but the title was subsequently chosen to indicate the link between these conferences on various subjects, since, as it happens, the theme of joy does, one might say "by chance," appear in all of them, despite the fact that a reader glancing at the chapter headings might well form the opinion that most of them present a somewhat grim appearance. But this only proves all the more

[2] Cf. Dom Morin, *The Ideal of the Monastic Life.*

vividly how universally joy does pervade the Christian religion, since it predominates even in those aspects of it which might be thought almost to exclude it.

The pages that follow have little claim to originality; at this stage in the world's history one cannot be original as regards the age-old truths of the faith. But the primary purpose of the book is to help other souls by putting before them considerations that have helped the writer. If it succeeds in doing that, the question of originality is of little importance, though whenever possible the original author of a statement has been indicated. It is the humble hope of the present writer that, by God's grace and mercy, these pages may bring some comfort and encouragement to souls striving to serve God faithfully, in which case he will have been highly privileged and rewarded.

CONTENTS

I

CHRIST WITHIN US

Our holy religion offers us innumerable causes of deep and abiding joy, joy which no tribulations, however great, can banish, for it is not dependent upon the changing circumstances of our lives. It is a joy which rests upon unshakable foundations. But one such cause in particular is of vital importance to our souls, and yet is unfortunately too often forgotten by many of us: this is the joy brought by the fact and the knowledge of the presence of God within us, the indwelling of the Most Holy Trinity in our souls. That most marvelous presence makes all the difference to us, for this it is that is the vitalizing principle of our souls, the very life of our life; whereas without it we are but dead shells, "walking corpses," as someone has expressed it.

It is the ardent desire and firm determination of all us religious that, with the help of God's grace, our lives shall be truly spiritual; but if that is to be so, we must be habitually mindful of God, having the continual thought of God with us, since by this means we grow in the knowledge and love of Christ and thereby more easily and readily come to know and to fulfill His holy will. For our entire purpose must be the fulfilling of the divine will: this is

1

everything to us. Hence God said to St. Catherine of Siena: "Know, therefore, that the salvation of My servants and all their perfection depend upon this one thing: that they do in all things My will only; and to that end, that every moment of their lives they use every effort to seek Me alone, to honor Me alone, to please Me alone. The more diligently they apply themselves to this, the nearer do they approach perfection, because by this means they draw nearer to Me." Thus we see that continual application to God is the necessary approach to holiness.

We all know that the ultimate object of life is that we should possess God for all eternity; but that this may be so, we must also possess Him in this life. We cannot have Him in the next world unless we have zealously and faithfully striven to make Him our own while still in this world. And in His mercy and love the divine Word has made this possible for us by His sacred incarnation and by His indwelling in those souls which are in the state of grace. By His incarnation He has, so to speak, become one of us, and that sacred body and blood which He then took to Himself He gives to us in our Holy Communion so that He becomes ours in the most intimate degree possible. And further, in accordance with His promise He ever dwells within us by grace as in an inmost sanctuary. St. Teresa, using her famous simile of an interior castle, tells us that the soul has many chambers, all of which surround a central point wherein is God Himself, and she adds that if she herself had earlier realized this great fact she would have taken greater pains to keep her soul free from all imperfections. We should reflect on this truth, for realization of it will give us immense help in persevering in our efforts to acquire holiness and to conquer ourselves.

Hence we should frequently advert to the presence of Christ within us, withdrawing our senses from outward things and, no matter how busy our lives may be, retreating into ourselves wherein is our own sanctuary. Indeed it is possible for each of us to make this sanctuary and to keep it inviolable, drawing from it strength, comfort, and guidance, since therein is our divine Companion, waiting for us to come to Him. Yet how often we forget altogether the existence of this shrine within us! How often we tend to think that we are left to fight our battles alone, while all the time our omnipotent Lover is within our very selves, waiting to be asked to give His help, His guidance, His support! There in that inmost fastness He is ever at our disposal and, if we speak to Him and listen to Him, we will speedily develop a real interior life. And without an interior life a religious is not a religious at all. On the other hand, it is when we assiduously cultivate this interior life that we answer the invitation of Scripture: "Taste and see how sweet the Lord is." This sweetness, its existence and its power, no one can realize until he has actually experienced it, and to this experience God urges us again and again. "Come unto Me, all ye who labor, and I will refresh you." And all this because the Most Blessed Trinity is actually within those souls that are in the state of grace. Did not the divine Lover say: "If anyone love Me, . . . My Father will love him, and We will come to him and make Our abode with him"? (John 14:23.) What a glorious and gracious promise this is! And it can be realized in each of us.

Thus it is, then, that through grace we have God within us at all times, so that we are, as St. Paul says, "temples of God." [1] Each soul in grace is a temple of the Holy Ghost, and therefore sacred; we are, in fact, living tabernacles, and that not only when we have for a brief time the body and blood of God within us after receiving Holy Communion, but at all times throughout our life through grace. We are, then, tabernacles or chalices, but, as Father Plus well points out, that is not enough; for we must not keep God to ourselves. He gives Himself to us so that we may show Him to all men: "So let your light shine before men that they may . . . glorify your Father who is in heaven" (Matt. 5:16). We must, then, show outwardly something of the joy and peace and holiness imparted to us by the divine Guest within. In other words, according to Father Plus, we must not merely be tabernacles or chalices, we must be monstrances.

And we may be quite sure that if we pay assiduous attention to the divine presence within us, we shall have a peace of heart which nothing else can give and which nothing can shake or take from us. This is the peace that "surpasseth all understanding," which is not at the mercy of external events, the peace that is the "pearl of

---

[1] "Know you not that you are the temple of God and that the spirit of God dwelleth in you?" (I Cor. 3:16.)

great price," and that constitutes in great part the hundredfold reward which our Blessed Lord has promised to His faithful followers. How should the presence of Christ bring other than peace? And what could more greatly encourage or strengthen us in our daily struggle to serve Him wholeheartedly than the possession of this priceless gift? As, according to the admonition of St. Francis de Sales, disturbing thoughts come from the devil, so peace and serenity come to us from Him who said: "Peace I leave with you; My peace I give unto you. Not as the world giveth, do I give unto you" (John 14:27). And we should realize that this peace does not reside in our feelings, but in the soul, which is independent of mere feelings; hence it is the more valuable and solid and enduring. Here, then, we have one of the main sources of the joy which comes from serving God; one which we can never sufficiently treasure, and for which we can never sufficiently thank God.

On the subject of this peace and of the accompanying sweetness which it brings, as also on the indwelling of Christ within us which is its source, we may find help and encouragement, as on many other aspects of the spiritual life, in the most beautiful and moving of all books, *The Imitation of Christ*. Thus, for instance, great solace is given us by the following passage dealing with this very subject: "Christ will come unto thee and show thee His consolation if thou prepare for Him a worthy mansion within thee. The inward man He often visiteth, and hath with him sweet discourses, pleasant solace, much peace, and familiarity exceeding wonderful. O faithful soul, make ready thy heart for this bridegroom that He may vouchsafe to come to thee and dwell within thee. For when thou hast Christ thou art rich and hast enough. He will be thy faithful and provident helper in all things." And further on we read: "Thou shalt never have rest unless thou be most inwardly united unto Christ." And thus we see once again that loving union with the Christ within us is the true approach to holiness. Moreover, as St. Teresa points out, there is in that method of approach nothing to fatigue the mind or to disturb the soul. On the other hand, it is a solid foundation on which God can build; and what a wonderful return is thereby secured for us at the cost of so slight an effort!

Now, in view of all this, is it not well worth our while to cultivate most carefully a realization of this presence within us? This is a practice which has been dear to all the saints: the practice of the presence of God, not only around us, but in us. It was, for instance, the lifelong devotion of the famous Carmelite, Brother Lawrence, whose little book on the subject is still of the utmost value. From this realization of the divine presence we cannot but draw help and strength, and it is a powerful incentive to our refraining from the slightest sin. It is well, then, to examine ourselves and to see whether we have been seeking God too much without and forgetting that He is all the time within.

In this connection, too, we need to remember that by our very nature we must have interest and consolation from some source, and if we do not find within us the source of our consolation and happiness we inevitably turn to seek it outwardly in the things of the world; for otherwise life becomes dull and drab and loses its savor; then discontent soon follows. Indeed, even if we do find happiness and distraction of a sort in worldly things, discontent and unhappiness will invariably and speedily follow, for these things can never really satisfy us. But this cannot be the case if we have our eternal Friend within us, and are accustomed to turn to Him there, not ignoring His sacred presence, but having habitual recourse to it. A keen realization of that presence within us revolutionizes our life and makes a great difference.

While I have been stressing this method of approaching and finding God, which has such valuable results and is at the same time so simple, I do not, of course, thereby in any way disparage the importance of the physical presence of our Blessed Lord in the Most Holy Sacrament of the Altar. That we must never neglect. The tabernacle must ever be the center of the life of every religious house, and to it we must have recourse ceaselessly. Such is God's will, because our nature needs His sacramental presence, and our affections respond more easily perhaps to His real though veiled appearance in our midst. But by the very nature of the case Our Lord is by this means within us only for a short while after we receive Holy Communion, whereas by grace He is always in us, so long as we do not drive Him out by mortal sin. And so, while loving and adoring our dear Lord in the

Blessed Sacrament, let us remember also that He is all the time within us. "The kingdom of God is within you" (Luke 17:21), says Holy Scripture. In fact, each of us must have either heaven or hell within him. There is no intermediate state, for the essence of hell is the absence of God. But the majority of mankind forget that truth and act accordingly. We, however, the chosen friends of God, know that He is always with us, always at our disposal, always strengthening and encouraging us. With that knowledge we can face all difficulties.

II

OBEDIENCE AND SILENCE

Although every virtue has its own particular attractiveness, those virtues that are peculiar to the religious life have a special beauty of their own. Anyone who has a vocation to that life is strongly drawn to them, even though he may not always perfectly practice them. For virtue is always attractive; monastic virtue is specially so. Now, there are two such monastic virtues [1] which always seem to have a special beauty: those of obedience and silence.

These two virtues which play such a prominent part in the lives of all religious have, in fact, several points in common. For one thing, both call for much self-control, especially with some people; for we have an instinct to talk, an instinct not confined to the gentler sex, despite a common notion to that effect. And we also have an instinct to do our own will. Hence in observing each of these virtues we have to practice rigid self-control. Then, too, both of these virtues bring much peace, to ourselves and to others; whereas any flouting of them nearly always causes trouble of some sort. Both, again, are valuable

[1] As regards silence, the word "virtue" is used in this conference, not in its theological sense; strictly speaking, silence is not a virtue. It is here called a virtue in the sense that it is meritorious in the religious life.

9

aids to virtue in general and to the molding of our characters. And lastly, both are comparatively easy to practice.

Let us first look at those features just mentioned so far as they are connected with obedience. The first was self-control. However much we value obedience, sometimes in our lives we are sorely tempted against it; times when we long to do our own will for once. Indeed nothing so disciplines the soul as constant and unswerving obedience. On this point listen to the late Bishop Hedley: "On obedience depends our religious spirit, and on our religious spirit depends life everlasting. Obedience is in itself religious perfection. To be genuine children of our heavenly Father we must be humble, and to make sure of continuous humiliation continuous obedience is the sovereign secret. Obedience," he goes on, "is also a sacrifice: the sacrifice of self-will, which is the most thorough sacrifice the human heart can make. . . . Even from the pure and innocent, God delights to receive the holocaust of their will. Why? Because the more they immolate their will, the more they strain out pride from their natures." Thus writes the holy bishop, and St. Bonaventure, for his part, tells us that "religious perfection consists totally in the renunciation of our own will."

Secondly, it brings peace. This truth is surely obvious, and it is also perhaps the most attractive result of obedience. Obedience brings peace because by it we know for certain that we are doing what is right. We know that we are thereby fulfilling God's will, and doing precisely what

He would have us do. We have not to decide our own course and thereby run innumerable dangers. We are infallibly put on the right course by obedience, and kept in it by obedience; and from that knowledge we have a deep and abiding peace. How fortunate we are in thus having the means of knowing for certain that we are, every minute of the day and night, doing God's will, and therefore doing what alone is worth doing, and what alone is meritorious!

The next point mentioned above was that obedience is a valuable aid to virtue; indeed it advances us rapidly toward perfection, for it is the only safe road. By reason of the rigorous discipline it imposes on our unruly wills it gives us the victory over self and over the devil, and moreover innumerable merits are accumulated by it. Every little thing that we do through religious obedience is an act of worship and is therefore meritorious in the eyes of God, no matter how trivial or indifferent it may be in the eyes of the world. For this reason no task or occupation in the religious life is altogether worthless. All alike are done for God and in fulfillment of His will, and are therefore pleasing to Him. The Prophet says: "An obedient man shall speak of victory" (Prov. 21:28); and every day we are truly victors, victors over ourselves and over the Evil One, by reason of our obedience. It is thus a most powerful protection against sin, since sin comes always from self-will and self-indulgence, and from these we are efficaciously shielded by holy obedience.

Lastly, we said that obedience is comparatively easy to observe. We have only to do what we are told. There is nothing very hard about that. As the young St. Peter of Luxemburg once said: "I shall always be an unprofitable servant, but I can at least obey." And in point of fact even things which appear difficult often become surprisingly easy when undertaken under obedience. But after all, that is what we might expect, because, if God gives us a thing to do, His justice leads Him to give us also the means and the grace with which to do it. Over and over again we read in the lives of the saints of almost impossible things being done by virtue of obedience, even of sick men rising from their beds at once when a superior commanded them to do so. The call of obedience has always powerfully helped religious. In this connection one may recall that in Queen Elizabeth's reign, when the English Bridgettine nuns were in exile at Rouen, some of them were sent over to England at peril of their lives to obtain postulants and to collect alms, and were mostly thrown into prison on arrival in England. One of them thus imprisoned at Winchester was Sister Elizabeth Sanders. After several months' imprisonment, upon hearing that her superior had ordered all her nuns in England to return to Rouen, she was so fired by love of obedience that she actually contrived at great risk to escape from the prison by climbing over the high wall in a man's disguise, and made her way after almost incredible adventures to the coast, where she was smuggled on board a vessel and so got back to Rouen.[2] Such is the call of obedience which makes us do things we would never dare to attempt on our own initiative.

All these qualities of obedience that we have been considering make it of very great value to us, and therefore it is an outstanding characteristic, indeed one of the essential foundations, of the religious life, and one that is insistently urged upon us in Sacred Scripture. The Bible starts with the story of the disobedience which brought sin into the world, and the Fathers repeatedly contrast Eve's disobedience with the unquestioning obedience of Mary to the will of God; and the whole life of our Blessed Lord Himself was one of unceasing obedience. He was subject to His parents as a child, and His sole purpose even as a man was to do the will of His heavenly Father: "I seek not My own will, but the will of Him that sent Me" (John 5:30); even in the Garden He cried out in anguish: "Father . . . not My will, but Thine be done" (Luke 22:42), so that He indeed was, as St. Paul says, "obedient unto death." Therefore the same apostle tells us not merely that we must obey our superiors, but he says: "Be ye subject to every creature." That is the way to root out self-will, and self-will is the cause of our troubles and failings.

But above all, as already mentioned, obedience is the sure way of doing God's will; and above all it is obedience that He asks of us. "Obedience is better than sacri-

[2] See the present writer's *Historic English Convents of To-day*.

fices" (I Kings 15:22), and the Franciscan lay brother, St. Pascal Baylon, was fond of saying: "Brother, obedience comes first; devotion must take second place." Yes, better obedience any time, than lengthy private devotions. And since it gives us the guaranty that we are doing God's will, it is the sure and safe way to heaven. And what a blessing it is to have this unfailing guidance! Therein lies the attraction of obedience. So closely should we love to adhere to it that a superior should have only to hint a desire or a wish, and we fulfill it at once without needing a command. For this reason, too, our obedience must be blind. That is of the essence of religious obedience, for we do not obey merely because we happen to approve of the reasons or motives behind an order; we obey simply and solely because we are told. Consequently we should never ask for reasons. To do so would be to spoil our obedience, to put a blemish on our offering to God. No, we must not act from self-will or from motives of private judgment. That would not be religious obedience at all. True obedience is blind.

In this connection I may remind you that St. Francis de Sales declares that loving obedience has three qualities: it is blind, it is prompt, and it is persevering. Being blind, he says, it never regards the personality or motives of the superior, but only his authority. In passing, let me stress that point, for it is of supreme importance. If we regard the person or motive of the superior, we shall never have peace, even though we may obey. In this matter we require simplicity, a simplicity which does not inquire into motives and reasons, and without which we cannot have that docility which is the way of happiness and holiness. So St. Francis says that true obedience does not regard the motive of a command, and he goes on to add that it never demurs or delays, and it never asks how it is to carry out the command, knowing that God will give the means since He inspired the command. "Behold the handmaid of the Lord": that must be our motto in this matter. Instant and precise obedience is our aim, and nothing is more pleasing to God or more profitable to ourselves. "Speak, Lord, for Thy servant heareth" (I Kings 3:9), said the child Samuel, and so also do we. If, unhappily, it should not have been true of us up to now, let us make certain that it will be true of us henceforth, and let us train ourselves to delight in this virtue.

And now what of its twin silence? It also has the same four characteristics mentioned in connection with obedience. Thus it often requires great self-control. Perhaps we are bursting with a piece of news which we feel we simply must impart to someone, and we find that it is the time of silence. Self-control is called for. It is a glorious opportunity of meriting and of obeying. Or it may be loneliness that is the matter, and we feel we must talk to someone; or it is a case of making a repartee, with a clever and crushing retort on the tip of our tongue. Silence! That is especially the time to practice it. In any event, when we come to look back on things, we may well realize that nine-tenths of our remarks in the past might just as well not have been said, and no one would have lost anything of value. "A religious," said a fifteenth-century writer, "should be as sparing of his words as a miser of his gold." Self-control, then, it calls for continually.

Secondly, it always produces peace just as obedience does, whereas talking frequently brings trouble. "A man who holds his peace about the affairs of others," it has been well said, "has peace with all men." Chattering disturbs our peace and our recollection as well as that of others. Moreover, we frequently have cause to regret things we have said, but we seldom have cause to regret silence. The tongue, indeed, is a fruitful cause of sins; but that thought cannot be expanded now. At any rate, we all know the prevalence of uncharitableness, and the many strong biblical texts on the subject. St. James says that if we bridle not our tongue, all our religion is in vain, and he calls the tongue "an unquiet evil, full of deadly poison" (Jas. 3:8). An occasional examination about whether we try sufficiently to govern the tongue, might surprise us in its results.

And so, silence is thirdly a valuable aid to virtue. In silence God speaks to the soul; whereas the interior spirit is much dissipated by talking. Our character, too, is molded by silence, and to be habitually silent can be a sign of strength, of self-control, whereas talking is frequently a sign of shallowness. "Still waters run deep," is an old and wise saying, and you probably remember the old rhyme which runs:

> A wise old owl once sat in an oak,
> The more it heard, the less it spoke;

The less it spoke, the more it heard.
Why can't we be like that wise old bird?

Why, indeed? Do not, then, be a chatterer or, still worse, a gossiper.

The practice of silence also has the fourth quality, that it is easy to acquire with a little perseverance. After all, it is only negative: it only implies refraining from doing something. But if we must talk, and there are times when it is our duty, as, for instance, during recreation, let us bear in mind the time-honored advice to speak of things and not of persons. It is surprising how often conversation turns to the subject of other people, and still more so how it nearly always is to their discredit. We seem instinctively to see the worst qualities in people, and so we discuss them. "Judge not, that you may not be judged" (Matt. 7:1). Thus self-control in speaking is necessary, not only for the preservation of the religious spirit, but even for that of the state of grace.

We can come to find great joy through silence, and great peace; it is not too much to say that the spirit of a religious house can be judged by the degree to which the rules of silence are observed. And we generally find that something we have refrained from saying was not, after all, worth saying when we consider it later. Often, as I have said, we feel we must say something during the time of silence, or in a place of silence; but if we refrain we frequently find that when recreation time comes we have forgotten what it was, and no one seems one whit the worse for our not saying it. Or else we discover that our titbit of news was already known; thus in any event it was not worth saying. "Experience proves," says St. Alphonsus, "that in convents where silence reigns the rules are well kept; whereas in those in which silence is not observed there is but little fervor." And if we love silence and obedience, we will be most careful to break off talking the moment we hear the bell that marks the end of recreation , even if it requires stopping in the middle of a sentence, and even though we may at first feel self-conscious in doing so. To do so will strengthen our own respect for silence, and will also set an excellent example. But let us take care that we do not pride ourselves on that last aspect of it.

In conclusion, let us strive to be exact in our observance of these two important mortifications: obedience and silence. Let us ask for grace to grow in the practice of them and in the love of them, and we shall find yet again the truth of the old adage: "Keep your Rule, and your Rule will keep you."

III

THE SACRED PASSION

It is well at times to consider fundamentals, which as a general rule we are too likely to take for granted. Let us, then, consider briefly the first Good Friday, one of the most momentous days in the history of the world, surpassed possibly or equalled in importance by Christmas or Easter, but by no other. Nor let it be thought incongruous that in a volume devoted to the subject of the joy derived from serving God we should dwell upon such a somber topic as the death of our Savior; for that event is the source from which ultimately all our joy comes, and the cause of the hope and the faith which is in us.

Do we always sufficiently realize that this day, the first Good Friday, witnessed that stupendous event, unique in the history of creation, the trial and death of God? How amazing it is that man should ever have done such a thing as to call God to judgment and to condemn Him to death, that the incarnate God should have submitted to it, and that it should have been love for such as we are that moved Him to submit to it! And now down the centuries there cries the voice of Christ, reminding us of what He has endured for our sakes. That voice rings in our ears for it is the voice of one who has experienced all the bitterness of ingratitude, although no bitterness is to be found in Him.

Indeed, for us, frail beings that we are, ingratitude can be the most embittering thing in life.

> Blow, blow, thou winter wind,
> Thou art not so unkind
> As man's ingratitude.

And yet, despite it all He loves us still, and as much as ever. Love indeed is the key to the Passion. "Having loved His own who were in the world, He loved them unto the end" (John 13:1); and He Himself tells us: "Greater love than this no man hath, that a man lay down his life for his friends" (John 15:13). This key reveals the depths of agony which lie beneath the story of the Passion, and of which we, while in this life, can only scratch the surface. It was the element of love in it that was stressed by Our Lord Himself and by the apostles. For love and suffering are ever united in this life, even though love brings with it joy. And as in human affairs love involves suffering, so is it in spiritual matters. Hence Christ's love leads Him to suffer for us, and hence, too, our love for Him leads us to suffer gladly, in our own small degree, for Him. But if love involves suffering, let us see to it that conversely our suffering involves love, that our mortifications and the privations which are so necessary and so prominent a part of the religious life spring from love and are sweetened by it. Love cannot be satisfied without suffering for the loved one, and we can find in suffering the joy of being able to prove our love. Love turns sorrow into joy; and, though suffering itself remains, it is welcomed. Indeed to those who love Him, God not only gives the grace to face suffering, but also the greater grace to desire it.

Is it not this that marks out the truly Christian life from every other? For life is transfigured when it is shot through with divine love. What a vast difference it makes to our whole outlook on life, what courage, what endurance, what joy, is poured into us, when we fully realize that suffering is the concomitant of love, that it is the expression of God's love for us, and that we can make it the expression of our overmastering love for God! Here is no stoic suffering for the mere sake of suffering, no self-infliction of pain for motives such as those which move the pagan philosopher or the heathen fakir. For us suffering is the expression of love: a new conception brought into the world by Christianity, and giving satisfaction to the deepest instincts of the human heart. And we know, too, that this privilege of sharing in the sufferings of Christ fulfills the twofold need of enabling us to make up "those things that are wanting of the sufferings of Christ" (Col. 1:24), that is, the cosuffering of us who are His members, and of fulfilling the condition on which alone we can attain by His grace and mercy to eternal felicity. St. Paul assures us that if we are to share in the glory of Christ, we must first share in His sufferings: "We are the sons of God, and if sons, heirs also; heirs indeed of God, and joint heirs with Christ:

yet so, if we suffer with Him, that we may be also glorified with Him" (Rom. 8:16 f.).[1] To this, indeed, we are imperatively called by the Master Himself: "If any man will come after Me, let him . . . take up his cross daily and follow Me" (Luke 9:23), while it is made plain to us that this is to be no mere barren asceticism, but one that is motivated by love, since He also assures us that His yoke is sweet and His burden, which He invites us to share, is light. This they could not be were they not borne through love and rendered even delightful through the transmuting influence of love. "Love makes all things easy."

But in the case of our Blessed Lord, His very perfection made His sufferings all the greater. For who can gauge how repulsive to the All-Holiest must have been the slightest trace of sin? Yet He was surrounded by it on all sides, and moreover He had ever present to Him the sins of the whole world from the beginning of time and stretching into the unlimited future. All these He saw as He lay and shuddered in the Garden that Thursday night; with Him the past, present, and future were and are all one since He is God, and the accumulated weight of iniquity crushed Him to the ground. Never were there sufferings such as His sensitive human nature had to endure from this source, while He also saw His apparent lack of success even with His own people: "He came unto His own; and His own received Him not" (John 1:11). In clear vision He likewise saw the hideous physical suffer-

---

[1] Or, as Knox's translation has it: "Heirs of God, sharing the inheritance of Christ; only we must share His sufferings, if we are to share His glory."

ings which were to be His upon the morrow, and which His divinity enabled Him to foresee in all their details. For three and thirty years He had labored and suffered for this people, and this was how they requited Him. He saw, too, the heart-break of His Blessed Mother, who was to witness His passion, and His desertion even by the apostles themselves whom He had Himself selected and to whom He had given everything. Truly the cup would be filled to the brim.

And yet, despite all this and much more that we cannot even imagine, despite the agony of fear that wrung from His heart the cry: "Father, if it be possible, let this chalice pass from Me" (Matt. 26:39)—despite all that, what are the words which echo in the Garden that night and which decide the future of all mankind? "Father . . . not My will, but Thine, be done" (Luke 22:42). And at the sound of that sacred voice pronouncing those fateful words, all creation bows down in awe. No need to remind you that it was we who caused that supreme agony in the heart of God, that it was our sins that brought the Omnipotent Divinity to this pass, or that the measure of His suffering gives us some faint idea of the intensity of the love that led Him to endure it on our behalf.

Yes, that is the key. His love could never die, and love conquers everything, so that His apparent failure was in reality His blazing triumph. Looking ahead He saw the pain and the grief which through untold ages to come would be turned into joy because of what He was now enduring, that joy which, as He foretold, "no man shall take from you" (John 16:22). And yet that love does but make the behavior of mankind, both then and now, so much the worse, so much the more incomprehensible, so that surely it was at that time as He lay prostrate in His agony that there must have come into His mind the heartbreaking Reproaches of the Good Friday liturgy: "O My people, what have I done to thee, or wherein have I grieved thee? Answer Me. Because I led thee out from the desert and brought thee into a land exceedingly good, thou hast prepared a cross for thy Savior. What more ought I to have done for thee and have not done it? But in My thirst thou hast given Me vinegar, and with a spear thou hast pierced My side. I fed thee with manna through the desert, and thou hast beaten Me with blows and stripes. I gave thee a royal scepter, and thou hast given to My head a crown of thorns. Jerusalem, Jerusalem, turn again unto thy God." And yet it was for this faithless people, for those who were to return Him evil for good, it was for all of us that He was to endure the ignominy, the mental and physical anguish of Calvary; it was for such as we are that He could say: "Father . . . I have finished the work which Thou gavest Me to do. . . . I will that where I am, they also whom Thou hast given Me may be" (John 17:4, 24).

But the essence of Good Friday and of the spirit shown by our Blessed Lord is summed up in that marvelous fifty-third chapter of Isaias. Bear with me while I quote the familiar words of that exact prophecy: "Despised and the most abject of men, a man of sorrows and acquainted with infirmity; and his look was as it were hidden and despised. . . . Surely he hath borne our infirmities and carried our sorrows, and we have thought him as it were a leper and as one struck by God and afflicted. But he was wounded for our iniquities; he was bruised for our sins. The chastisement of our peace was upon him, and by his bruises we are healed. . . . And the Lord hath laid on him the iniquity of us all. . . . He shall be led as a sheep to the slaughter . . . and he shall not open his mouth." Might not all this almost have been written by St. Paul years after the event, rather than by Isaias centuries before it? And who can listen to it unmoved, and without taking a resolution never to add another bruise to our dear Lord by sin? Yes, that is the whole point; for there is little use in meditating on the sacred Passion, little use in commiserating Our Lord's sufferings, or even in thanking Him for them, if we do not at once give our reflections and emotions a practical turn, so that they have henceforth a real effect on our mode of life. God does not ask for sentiment from us, nor yet for our pity; He does ask and demand that we put into practice the holy inspirations which He sends to us and that we ceaselessly strive to model our lives on the example He set us while on earth, and thereby prove the reality of our love.

"Having loved His own who were in the world, He loved them unto the end" (John 13:1). It is hard to think of words more tender than some of the last recorded sayings of Jesus. No one can be unmoved by: "I will not now call you servants. . . . But I have called you friends.

. . . You have not chosen Me; but I have chosen you.
. . . You are they who have continued with Me in My temptations. . . . I will not leave you orphans; I will come to you. . . . I will come again and will take you to Myself. . . . Peace I leave with you; My peace I give unto you. . . . As the Father hath loved Me, I also have loved you. . . . Ask, and you shall receive, that your joy may be full." There is an almost unbearable tenderness in these and many other phrases from His lips; it is as though He could not cease murmuring endearments and encouragement, and this even on the very eve of the day on which His faithless children, as He well knew, would betray Him and crucify Him.

Such is the Lord we serve, such the Master we love. Is it, then, any wonder that it has been said that "the great ones of the earth lie forgotten and unloved, while Jesus has had, and will have to the end of time, more devout followers than the stars in the heavens or the sands of the seashore"? Happy are we to have the inestimable privilege of being numbered not merely among those followers, but, by reason of our vows, in the picked band of His most intimate companions. Such are we now, thanks to His forbearance and to His grace. God grant that we may also be in that band for all eternity, after a life of loving and faithful service; and that by these our lives we may be privileged to make some amends for the wounds inflicted on that Master by the thoughtlessness and malice of a foolish and sinful world.

IV

MENTAL PRAYER

We religious must never forget that we are bound by our state to tend toward perfection and to aim ceaselessly at it. Indeed, St. Jerome goes so far as to say that a religious who does not strive for perfection is guilty of apostasy. But if we are to approach perfection, the practice of daily mental prayer is absolutely necessary for us. It keeps us in touch with God and is, in fact, the breath of life to our souls, so that holiness is impossible without it. Well, then, might St. Teresa of Avila say: "He who gives up mental prayer does not require the devil to push him into hell; he goes there of his own accord." What it comes to is that we need to cultivate prayerfulness, which is the essence of the spiritual life, and prayerfulness is acquired chiefly by mental prayer and spiritual reading. It is also greatly fostered by simplicity, that most important virtue for the monk or nun, which means, among other things, forgetfulness of self and the fostering of a truly religious spirit. And it is further helped by mortification, for the body and its senses, with their incessant and insatiable demands, call us from God. Nor should we forget in this connection the value of frequent aspirations in this nurturing of prayerfulness. Mother

27

Margaret Hallahan, the great restorer of the Dominican nuns in England, was so proficient in making aspirations and in preserving her prayerfulness in the midst of a multitude of occupations that she could say the Little Office of the Immaculate Conception while apparently conversing with a too long-winded person who would otherwise be causing her to waste her time. And indeed the various means just mentioned will enable us to fulfill St. Paul's injunction, to "pray always."

But now, we should realize that many persons, having a wrong idea of prayer, fancy it is difficult. Prayer should not be difficult; it should come to us as naturally as breathing, for it springs from our very nature. As the flower turns naturally to the life-giving sun, so our souls turn naturally to God, who is their life. The point to remember in this connection is that prayer is simply the raising of the heart and mind to God. Anything that enables us to do that is a method of prayer, and a very excellent method. With many, and especially with Protestants, prayer is solely the prayer of petition. They associate prayer almost exclusively with asking for favors. But what a false idea this is! Far more important is the prayer of adoration or that of thanksgiving. What must God think of us if we never approach Him except when we ask Him for something? Prayer means union with God. That is all. And anything that promotes such union is prayer. But if we are to have this union, a certain amount of what is called remote preparation is necessary. We must, for instance, try to have habitual recollection, for we cannot commune

with God if our heart and mind are habitually filled with
worldly matters, and we must learn to view things from
God's standpoint [1] and, moreover, have purity of intention. In a word, we must try to live with God and for
God.

As for prayer itself: the golden rule, as someone has
said, is that there is no golden rule; we must each use
whatever way suits us best. For temperaments and abilities vary enormously, and the method which suits one
soul will be impossible for another. But there is one thing
that applies to us all: prayer is not a matter of the feelings
but of the will (the same, of course, is true of sin); therefore coldness and dryness do not matter when they are
not our own fault, except that, in a sense, they make our
prayer even more meritorious than if we were fervent,
because in such prayer self-indulgence cannot creep in,
and it calls for a real effort on our part. That is why God
often prefers to find coldness and dryness in us, and indeed sends them to us. As St. Catherine of Genoa remarked: "He loves us to come to His feet with reluctance,"
for then it is a pure exercise of the will, and we are not
doing it for what we can get out of it, but solely in order
to please God. In those circumstances, when we feel we
cannot pray, we should not forget that we are praying
by the mere fact of our presence in the church coupled
with our desire and intention of praying. We are in the
audience chamber and are attentive to God's words. We
are praying. If we can do nothing else, we can at least

[1] See chap. 12, *infra.*

force ourselves to sit or kneel there. That is one reason why it is absurd for people to say that they cannot pray. They say so simply because they have a wrong idea of what constitutes prayer. We have no need to say any words whatever to God. It is the heart that prays, not the mouth or the intellect. Nothing is easier, nor is there anything more important; it is the only way we can keep our spiritual engines running.

Now, the mental prayer of most of us is either meditation or else it is affective prayer; these two are not the same, for they use different faculties. The soul acts in two ways: by the understanding and by the will. By the one we reflect, probe, and examine; by the other we adore, thank, and love. Connected with the first of these is the imagination, and with the second the feelings; both can play an important part in our prayer, especially when the will begins to flag. But of all these things only the will is essential to prayer. There is no prayer without that. In meditation, for instance, we use the imagination and the understanding, but only in order to make the will produce acts or aspirations; if we stop short at the imagination or the understanding, without producing these acts, then we are not praying but merely reasoning. Let us not mistake the means for the end: the process of meditation for prayer itself.

As regards the use of these two different methods of prayer, it may in general be said that to those who are more advanced or who have spent many years in the religious life, the exclusive use of meditation (the imagination and the understanding) is liable to be merely a harmful distraction; while even for those who are less advanced, practice makes the moving of the will or heart easy without having recourse to such aids, although this facility needs assiduous cultivation. Before very long we find that the slightest effort will bring the affections into play without any course of reasoning. A Carthusian monk once told me he could never make the Stations of the Cross because as soon as he started at the first station he became lost in contemplation and was absorbed perhaps for hours without having realized the passage of time. That is an extreme example of the facility that comes to some. As a rule it is necessary for beginners to start with meditation, but after a few years of religious life most people pass from it, or should do so. We should not be in too great a hurry to leave meditation; but, on the other hand, we must not resist if God calls us to a higher form of prayer, as is generally the case when we find that meditation has become unduly difficult. If the acts can be produced without meditation, obviously it is so much the better, since the whole object of the meditation is simply to produce the acts. It follows, incidentally, that, if we use a book for our mental prayer, we should do so only sparingly; otherwise it becomes simply spiritual reading.

But some souls need to remain at the stage of meditation for many years, and if that should be the case with you, do not be disturbed by it, as it is God's will, and He will advance you to another form of prayer when it is for your own good. Yet even in meditation do not depend on the understanding too much. You may remember that St. Teresa of Avila, great mystic though she was, experienced for fourteen years such a state of aridity that she had to use a book for her meditation; and yet she herself said:"Let the soul not trouble herself with the understanding, which is only a noise-maker"; and she also said: "The understanding is like a drone bee, which buzzes about the hive, and makes itself very important from its size, but produces no honey." In this connection we may add that, if you find that you cannot get the will or the affections to work without employing the understanding, there is a useful middle course possible, that of informal meditation. By this I mean the cultivation of the sense of God's presence, which is a useful practice also in other respects. He is present in three different ways: by His essence and by His power, by both of which He is present everywhere; and by His indwelling through grace in our souls, as has been previously explained.[2] It is of this last that we should think when we are trying to pray. Concentrate on the presence of God within you, remembering the text: "We [the Holy Trinity] will come to him, and will make Our abode with him" (John 14:23). It is from this indwelling that we derive our spiritual life, as the branches derive their life from the tree. "I am the vine; you the branches" (John 15:5); and souls in grace show forth the reflected beauty of the divine presence. God loves to dwell in us in this manner: "My delights were to be with the children of men" (Prov.

[2] See chap. 1, *supra.*

8:31). Let Him, then, come in; or rather go and visit Him already dwelling within you. That visit will be excellent prayer, since it is close communion with God, and then will you be able to say: "I to my beloved, and my beloved to me" (Cant. 6:2).

Mention of this mode of prayer naturally brings us to a consideration of contemplation, which may be either ordinary or extraordinary, that is, either acquired by our own efforts, or infused directly by God. Of these the former is possible for all with practice; the latter cannot be acquired, being a gratuitous gift of God, which should not be asked for, since it is an extraordinary favor. Here we are dealing only with ordinary contemplation, which, let us repeat it, is within the reach of all, and to which a variety of names is given: acquired contemplation, affective prayer, prayer of loving union, prayer of simplicity, and the like. In this prayer one remains almost passive, and confines oneself to keeping the attention fixed, though without any straining or violent effort, since it is important to avoid striving or violence. Be calm and passive. Meditation is active, contemplation is passive; in it we leave God to act, our part being to empty ourselves, as it were, and to keep the will fixed, making from time to time such acts, if any, as may come to us. Hence there is no suspicion of quietism in this form of prayer. But to strive or strain defeats our purpose by disturbing the mind. An admirable description of this form of prayer was given by St. John Vianney, the Curé of Ars, when he advised that in prayer you should, as he said, "shut your eyes, shut your mouth, open your heart," and it might also be added: "Shut your mind." For there should be no brainwork, not even about God; since what we seek is not to think about God (that is meditation), but to let God permeate us, to enable Him to operate in us. Abbot Chapman once made the striking statement: "Thinking is fatal in prayer." In vocal prayer we speak to God, but in mental prayer He speaks to us, if we let Him. The Psalmist says: "In my mediation a fire shall flame out" (Ps. 38:4). It is then that God pours Himself into us. Persevere at this, for it is well worth it, at times making aspirations or simple petitions when moved to, or when the will flags. Some such short phrase as "Holy, Holy, Holy, Lord God Almighty," or "My God and my All," or, perhaps best of all, "God alone," can keep us going for a long time.

Always remember, we should not violently resist distractions, but at most merely put them quietly and firmly away. It may well be that God wishes you to have them, since involuntary distractions are by no means entirely harmful. They can be great helps to humility and resignation; so long as they are not voluntary they cause no loss of the fruits of impetration or of merit.

What has been said, then, comes to this: simply rest in God's arms. You may remember the old peasant mentioned in the biography of the Curé of Ars. He spent hours daily before the Blessed Sacrament, and, when asked what he did during that time, replied that he did nothing, adding: "I look at Him, and He looks at me."

There you have supreme prayer. St. Teresa of Lisieux could not use set prayers, and with her, she tells us, prayer was "an outburst of the heart, anything that raises the soul to God." When particularly dry, she would simply say the Our Father or the Hail Mary very slowly, reflecting on each phrase. We need to put aside elaborate systems, which only worry us and, as a holy writer has advised, "try basking in the sun of God's love, quietly kneeling before the tabernacle as we would sit in the sunshine, not trying to do anything but love Him; but realizing that we are all the time at His feet, and especially when we are dry and cold, grace is dripping down on our souls, and we are thereby growing in holiness." For this reason Father Doyle says: "Every moment of prayer, especially before Him in the tabernacle, is a sure, positive gain." The best of all prayers is to kneel quietly and let Jesus pour Himself into our souls.

Because of all this many spiritual writers say to us: "Never meditate." The Carthusians, those great masters of the spiritual life, never set aside a time for meditation. That is because they know that any elevation to God is prayer, for example, manual labor in silence, such as that of the Cistercians, a silence impregnated with the presence of God. If all our work is thus dedicated to God, we are praying all day.

We have seen that this prayer of passive simplicity which we have been considering is affective prayer, sometimes called the prayer of abandonment; and we have also seen that it consists in a loving union of our will with the will of God, and in acts of the will when it is not simply passive. It is for those who do not need much preparation to make the will work. But, because of the need for humility and for avoiding singularity, we should make the ordinary preparation first. And this method of prayer has great merit, because the will alone is its principle and it is ruled by love. It also helps us to avoid distractions (an important consideration), for we are more moved by pious affections than by the understanding. We have, in fact, an instinct for God, and we have only to give it rein and to let God work in us. But whatever form of prayer we adopt, let us be sure we do it always to the best of our ability; for mental prayer is of the utmost value. The time we spend in having our daily audience with God is the most precious of the whole day. The learned theologian Suarez so greatly esteemed it that he said: "I would not exchange one quarter of an hour of mental prayer for all the knowledge I have acquired in so many years of study." And, incidentally, it is the more necessary the more active our form of life is. Persevere, then, patiently and without eagerness or worry, and especially make acts of the will; God will prosper your efforts.

V

DETACHMENT

You may recall the account of Elias, that, when he had been fasting for forty days in the wilderness and had come to the holy mount of Horeb, he was told to listen to the Lord. And first he heard a great and furious wind which even overturned the rocks; but the Lord, we are told, was not in the wind. And then there came an earthquake; but the Lord was not in the earthquake. Finally there came the breath of a gentle air; and when he felt that, Elias covered his face with his mantle, and the Lord God spoke to him (III Kings 19:11 ff.). It was in the peace and quiet of a gentle breath of air that God spoke to the prophet. So also is it with us. The Lord is not in upheavals and frenzies, but in tranquillity. When our souls are disturbed and storms rage within us, God does not speak to us. His is a still, small voice, and peace within is needed if we are to hear Him. That is one reason why we must not let ourselves give way to interior disturbance. If we remain in peace, we shall hear God's voice.

Now, peace of spirit and peace of mind are needed for the religious life if we are to live it profitably; only when we have those can we give ourselves entirely to God and hearken to His voice within us. Since disturbance of any kind separates us from God, the devil always is the father of disturbance. That, too, is why we must cultivate the spirit of detachment, or rather, it is one of the many strong reasons why we must do so; of the other reasons something will be said further on in this chapter.[1] We have already seen something of the beauty and attractiveness of silence and obedience.[2] But a third virtue equally attractive is detachment, for, if we are detached from worldly things, if, that is, we have a holy indifference, then nothing can upset us. We shall always be happy and at peace. And that is surely the explanation of the look of peace which one so often sees on the faces of religious. They have acquired a holy indifference, since they wish only the will of God to be done, and thus the buffets of life no longer disturb them. They bear out the truth of Father Faber's words: "There are no disappointments to those whose wills are buried in the will of God."

As usual, Thomas à Kempis has put the matter admirably: "As much," he says, "as a man loveth any worldly thing more than it should be loved, so much his mind is hindered from the true love he should have for God. If thou wert well purged from all inordinate affections, then whatsoever should befall thee would go to thy spiritual profit, and to the great increasing of grace and virtue in thy soul. But the cause why so many things displease thee and trouble thee, is that thou art not yet perfectly dead to the world, nor art thou yet fully severed from the love

[1] See also *infra,* chaps. 9 and 13.
[2] See *supra,* chap. 2.

of earthly things. If thou no longer dependest for comfort on worldly things, thou mayest behold more perfectly heavenly things, and thou shalt then continually sing to God with great joy and inward gladness of heart."

Those are words of great wisdom, pointing out to us the infallible path to peace, that most desirable possession. In a word, it is to be obtained by holy indifference, which itself comes only through self-discipline, implying rigorous and persistent self-conquest. Thus we have another reason for fighting against ourselves, in addition to the reason supplied by our desire to avoid sin. We have to root out our dependence on and enslavement to daily events and circumstances. This liberation is accomplished by mortification and especially by seeking God's will only, a rule of life as simple as it is attractive. Yet, as Mother Eugénie de Brou pointed out, this rule, which is so simple in theory, "implies in practice by an unavoidable consequence continual and never-ending sacrifice. Our Savior has said it. To follow Him, to do the will of God as He has done it, we must renounce self, fight incessantly that ingrained instinct of humanity which inclines each of us to center all on self."

Now, the opposite of this self-centeredness is abandonment to God. You have probably read several of Père de Caussade's books on abandonment. They describe a marvelously attractive doctrine. He sums up the whole spiritual life in abandonment: total abandonment of self. Not that there is anything new in that, but he has particularly stressed it. Many other writers, both before and since his time, have said much the same thing in different ways. Lacordaire declared: "We must have an absolute, unlimited certainty that whatever comes from God is best, even if from the human point of view it should seem to us to be the very worst." St. Francis de Sales similarly advises: "Abandon to the providence of God whatever you find difficult, and firmly believe that He will safely guide you, your life, and your affairs." Caussade, for his part, wrote: "Our concern is to please God only; if He is content, that is enough for us; all the rest is a mere nothing. In a few days we shall make our appearance before this great God, this infinite Being. Of what use (and for all eternity) will anything be that was not done for His sake and animated by His grace and spirit? If this truth were a little more familiar to us, what peace of neart and mind should we not enjoy already in our present life?"

Truly this power of abandoning ourselves to God is a great gift and an invaluable possession. I cannot forbear, even at the risk of unduly multiplying quotations, from giving you the words of Mother Janet Stuart, the great superior of the Sacred Heart nuns, to one in time of trial, for they well illustrate this abandonment in actual practice. "Trust Him," she wrote; "He knows what He is doing, and you must have absolute confidence in Him, whatever you feel. And when you can do nothing else, shut your eyes and fall back on the simple affirmation which contains all else: I believe in God the Father Almighty. You need not say more, you need not feel even so much as that, but it is true, and the consequence of that truth is that in the words of Juliana of Norwich: All shall be well, and all shall be well, and thou shalt see that all things shall be well. Don't argue, don't fight inside, but just agree with God in will, though you do not see what He is going to do. He will never leave you alone. When He seems furthest He is quite near and full of sympathy, and knowing and understanding just what it feels like, having tasted of all these things Himself: fear, loneliness, weariness, questioning of what it is all to lead to: He knows it all, and His passing through it has left the grace for you, and you will come out of it a more seasoned soldier of Christ, and understanding more of His love and suffering than before,— and isn't that worth much?"

And when we have thus abandoned ourselves to God and in some measure acquired holy indifference, then we can understand those words: "All shall be well, and thou shalt see that all things shall be well." For to a soul thus trained and disciplined all things are necessarily well. Of course this involves seeing everything from the spiritual angle and not with the eyes of the world, and that is why a spiritual soul heartily distrusts human prudence and worldly wisdom. Moreover our Blessed Lord Himself has said that worldly wisdom is folly in the eyes of God, and that our ways are not His ways. Hence St. Francis de Sales cautions us: "Beware of human prudence, which our Savior reckons foolishness." Indeed on one occasion when he himself was urged to go to law to recover some property, he said: "No, indeed I will not. To him that would take away thy cloak give thy coat also. What is the good of so much concern for so transitory a life? Oh, I fear natural prudence extremely," he went on, "in the discernment of the things of grace, and if the prudence of the serpent be not diluted with the simplicity of the love of the Holy Spirit, it is altogether poisonous. . . . This prudence is opposed to that sweet repose which the children of God should have in heavenly Providence. Our outlook is either supernatural or it is good for nothing. We must remain in peace, in sweetness, in humility, in charity unfeigned, without complaining, without moving the lips. Oh, if we can have a spirit of entire dependence on the paternal care of our God, we shall with sweetness see the flowers multiply in other gardens, and shall bless God for it as if it were in our own."

There we have the ideal picture of holy indifference. Can we not at least strive to attain to it, if only for our own sakes? And, apart from our desire for peace of mind, to which allusion has already been made, three main reasons underlie this search for detachment. In the first place a soul closely united to God and really in love with God finds nothing earthly of sufficient interest to attract her. When one is permeated with God and with the things of the spirit, everything else seems but trivial. Accordingly such a soul cannot be perturbed by baubles and transient trifles, however important they may seem to be in the eyes of the world. Secondly, such a soul has this detachment because it wishes only the will of God to be done, and therefore does not fret, whatever may happen, but sees the finger of God in it and so rests content. And the third reason is that union with God, holiness, is altogether impossible without it. We cannot adhere firmly to God if we are still at the mercy of events and circumstances as regards our happiness and peace of mind; just as God cannot have possession of our hearts so long as they are still partially set on worldly things. These, then, are the reasons why a spiritual person has detachment, and they are three solid, common-sense reasons.[3]

A vivid picture of such a soul has been given by a French priest in these words: "It is in this sanctuary of peace where eternal silence dwells that the Almighty enters with delight; it is there He remains in security, and there He also operates without resistance. He seeks after the peaceful of heart, He communicates with them, and replenishes them with His spirit. They are children of His special predilection. The man of peace, who is freed from the tyranny of insatiable desires and anxious cares, enjoys an ineffable calm which gives him such a foretaste of eternal beatitude as he would not barter for all the gratification of sense. Under all circumstances such a soul is equally in peace, because all things are equal in her eyes, since she is persuaded that all are equally nothing. Her interior calm is beyond the reach of any incident."

Such, then, is the indifference that shows a detached soul, and such the peace that she enjoys. But, on the other hand, a soul that is not detached is disturbed by every ill chance, every reverse, and by everything that is contrary

[3] See also the magnificent and inspiring chapter on abandonment in Abbot Marmion's *Christ the Ideal of the Monk*.

to her likes or wishes. Such a soul is in perpetual turmoil and trouble, and therefore is distracted from God, so that much harm is done to her. For mental commotion and turmoil always harm the soul and separate her from God. That is why St. Francis de Sales says: "Every troubling thought is from the devil"; and similarly St. Alphonsus remarks: "No kind of disquietude, although for a good end, comes from God."

Now you can easily see that the logical result of this detachment and indifference is absolute obedience, acquiescence, lack of self-seeking, and a complete trust in and docility toward one's superior as representing God. It all comes down to trust in God, a trust that is put into practice and governs all our thoughts and actions. We recall Adelaide Proctor's lines:

Plan not nor scheme, but calmly wait:
  His choice is best;
While blind and erring is thy sight,
  So trust and rest.
Desire not; self-love is strong
  Within thy breast,
And yet He loves thee better still;
So let Him do His holy will,
  And trust and rest.

That, though perhaps not great poetry, admirably sums up the matter.

We need, then, to set ourselves a high standard in this, as in everything else. We dare not be content in spiritual matters with ordinary standards. Cardinal Vaughan once said: "Everyone consciously or unconsciously has a standard; and such is human nature that no one rises above his standard, but usually falls below it." Therefore aim high, set about acquiring perfect indifference and detachment, and the peace of God that passeth all understanding will be yours. This requires a stern struggle at first, but such a struggle is necessary in the religious life. We simply cannot, without treachery to God and grave danger to our salvation, stagnate or rest content without making an effort to improve.

We will conclude on that note by listening to St. Jane Frances de Chantal speaking to the community of which she was the founder and first superior. "If there is anyone," she said, "in the convent who lacks the courage to seek perfection whole-heartedly and give up being slack and uncertain, I pray that God may direct her return to the world. Here she can do no good either to herself or to religion. For myself, I would rather be frozen as a worldling than lukewarm as a religious. It is impossible that you should reach heaven unless you do violence to yourselves. Our Lord has said it Himself. I remind you of it that you may stamp upon your hearts an absolute resolve never to spare yourselves, but to conquer and crush out self in all things at whatever cost to your natural desires. Yet you must be gentle in your violence. You must give no quarter, you must slay. The spirit of the world and the flesh cannot combine with the spirit of religion. You must give up all your natural affections, your own judgment, your own will. These are the three things that are hardest to give up, and the three that are most essential. You must yield yourself so completely into the hands of those who direct you, that they can twist you as they will, as they might twist a handkerchief." So speaks the saint, and the disciple of the gentle yet firm St. Francis de Sales; and that attitude which she so vigorously portrays will both come from detachment and help us to a yet greater detachment.

VI

HUMILITY

Many lessons have to be learnt in the religious life, and most of them by making courageous persevering efforts. Every convent or monastery is a battlefield on which the spirit wars against the flesh and the devil; it is by no means a place of repose, even internally, much less externally. Yet most of these battles concern what are apparently simple and elementary things, and things which are of obvious benefit to us. None the less these battles are generally hard to win, and victory is the reward only of prolonged and determined effort.

An instance of this truth is afforded by the virtue of humility. That we must be humble is one of the most fundamental lessons to be mastered in the religious life, and it is a hard lesson for all, even for those who are temperamentally of a yielding and unself-assertive disposition; for pride can be worked on from many angles, in many different matters, and in diverse ways, and above all it has the disconcerting characteristic of bobbing up again when we genuinely think we have at last got the better of it. It would, in fact, be rash ever to think that we have eradicated pride; indeed, to think so would be itself pride, or perilously near it. It has a way of avenging itself on us for the slights and repressions put upon it, by showing itself alive at most unexpected times and in unexpected circumstances.

And still, how well worth-while it is to strive for it, for our Blessed Lord makes it a necessity for our salvation: "Unless you . . . become as little children, you shall not enter into the kingdom of heaven" (Matt. 18:3). But it is a stiff battle, because, though humility becomes strengthened by practice, it is extremely rare for it to be possessed completely. Yet the more we humble ourselves, the more ready God is to hear us. St. Peter says: "God resisteth the proud, but to the humble He giveth grace . . ." (I Pet. 5:5); and in fact the truly humble soul is a perfect one as a rule, so far as perfection is possible to mortals. And therefore humiliation has been held by ascetical writers to be the most valuable thing that the world contains, and a humiliation has been likened to a caress from the wounded hand of Christ. To a considerable extent we can measure how far we have succeeded in mastering our natural self by the degree of humility we have acquired.

But it is also of great use as a source of the other virtues, such as peace, charity, and fortitude. Consider these for a moment. Peace of mind is a most precious possession, and when it is lost in the religious life it is often because of a lack of humility, for pride is a gnawing and a nagging tyrant. Some one has been preferred before us for a certain task or post, our good qualities are not sufficiently recognized by superiors or equals, or perhaps some more subtle form of pride is present. All such things poison the mind and banish peace from it, so that it has been well said that "a little humility would save us a great deal of pain." Moreover, we know how necessary internal peace is if we are to make progress in the spiritual life.

In this connection let me give you some resolutions that were drawn up for himself on this subject by the famous Jesuit, Father William Doyle: "I get irritated and annoyed over trifles. In this connection I feel Jesus urges me to these things: 1. to take every single detail of my life as done by him (for example, all these causes of annoyance); 2. to accept it all lovingly in the spirit of immolation, so that my will and wishes may be annihilated; 3. never to complain or grumble even to myself; 4. to try to let everyone do with me as he pleases, looking on myself as a slave to be trampled on. If I kept these rules I should never be annoyed or upset about anything, and should never lose my peace of soul." [1] Notice that last sentence.

Those resolutions are based on humility; and habitual humility will indeed give this peace of mind and soul. We will then cease to resent any treatment whatever, knowing it to be fully deserved if the truth about us were really known, even though it may be unjust in the particular case in question. We will even rejoice in it for many reasons: among others, the fact that we will thereby be imitating Christ, receiving a salutary help toward per-

[1] Alfred Rahilly, *Father William Doyle, S.J.*

fection, mortifying ourselves. And all this on the principle of the old ascetic who said: "He who praises me, scourges me." Reflect on that saying and on the reasoning that lies behind it. When we can thus welcome all humiliations (and some can come in subtle forms), then shall we have full peace of mind.

But humility is also a source of charity. Do not quarrels, criticisms, strained relations, and the rest of that miserable brood, all come from self-love, from self-assertion, from, in fact, pride? The refusal to sink our own opinions or wishes, the complacent consideration of how much better we are than others in any given matter: these are the sources of criticisms and disputes from which we would be saved by a deep, convinced, and habitual humility. After all, as someone has said, "humblemindedness is truthfulness of mind." Yes, humility tells us the truth. We have to realize that God sees things quite differently from the way we see them, and He is not deceived by shams. He knows our worthlessness and our innumerable failures, and we should ask for the precious gift of seeing ourselves as we really are. Now, humility is the first essential for this clearsightedness, which in turn will itself increase our humility. That is why Jesus has said: "Learn of Me, because I am meek, and humble of heart; and you shall find rest to your souls" (Matt. 11:29); incidentally thereby confirming the truth that humility brings peace as well as charity. This humility will not only make us unwilling to judge others (in view of our own short-

NOW. I

comings), but will also make us less likely to cause friction by self-assertion and petty pride.

I have also said that humility is a source of fortitude, and here we meet one of the many paradoxes of Christianity. By our very littleness we grow strong. The world holds that self-confidence and self-reliance are requisite for success; and so they are—for worldly success. But they are ruinous to spiritual success, which, on the contrary, rests on a knowledge and conviction of our own weakness and failings. By the very knowledge of our weakness we are made strong, since it leads us to rely entirely on God, which is what St. Paul meant when he said: "Power is made perfect in infirmity" (II Cor. 12:9). In fact we are told by Holy Writ that "the weak things of this world hath God chosen that He may confound the strong" (I Cor. 1:27). It is when we can sincerely cry out each morning: "O Lord, do not leave me to myself today, or I am sure to betray Thee," that we can have confidence of receiving divinely given strength. Thus our very weakness becomes a source of strength, so that humility, which is nothing but the practical acknowledgment of our utter dependence on God, becomes the surety of our success. This, presumably, was what was in Chesterton's mind when he wrote that "humility is the mother of giants"; and he went on to add: "One sees great things from the valley, but only small things from a peak." Moreover we can with God's help rise to great things if we realize that we are starting from the valley, whereas if we fancy we

are already on a peak we shall rise no higher. It is only to
the humble that God gives His help. Humility, therefore,
is the indispensable preliminary to the acquisition of
strength.

Notice, however, that all this is distinct from false
humility, which is the kind commonly met with in the
world. This type of humility denies the possession of
qualities or abilities which are in fact possessed. It is
false modesty, and in reality a subtle form of pride. And
it is more contemptible than ordinary pride because it
is less open. Even if such a person is not actually fishing
for compliments, which he often is, his attitude arises
from a desire to be thought well of by others, to be considered modest and unassuming. Therefore it is pride,
and of no value in God's eyes. Moreover it is a poor way
of showing gratitude to God for the gifts He has given us,
to deny that we possess them. It is also a lie, and one
made for an unworthy purpose. Therefore let us not deny
our genuine powers, but at the same time have no pride
in them, realizing that they are a gift from God and are not
due to anything in ourselves; and if we are praised for
our good qualities or abilities, then we should give credit
to God and thank Him for them. "Not to us, O Lord, not
to us: but to Thy name give glory" (Ps. 113:1). That is
the true Christian attitude to one's talents and good qualities, and it is what St. Paul inculcates when he writes:
"What hast thou that thou hast not received, and if thou
hast received, why dost thou glory as if thou hadst not
received it?" (I Cor. 4:7.) In other words, all those things

which we are so proud of come to us gratuitously from God, and therefore we have nothing to be proud of in them. That is plain common sense. But human beings are often queer irrational creatures, especially where their pride is concerned, and we continue to take credit for and to glory in our few good qualities or talents as though they were entirely due to our own efforts.

Well now, realizing these facts, we will be in a better condition to fulfill St. Paul's exhortation to the Philippians: "Let nothing be done through contention, neither by vainglory. But in humility, let each esteem others better than themselves" (Phil. 2:3). There he mentions the two things that are contrary to humility, as arising from pride. Contention, even in trifling matters of opinion, is a sign of pride because the humble always yield. The Book of Proverbs says: "Among the proud there are always contentions"; and St. James says: "Where envying and contention is, there is inconstancy and every evil work" (Jas. 3:16). So, too, with the second evil mentioned by St. Paul, vainglory. This drives us to desire to be thought well of by others and to be respected. It is, in fact, the pharisaical attitude, and it can be a nagging devil in the mind, giving no rest. If it is not firmly eradicated, it grows insidiously; and if it is to be eradicated, our humility must be ceaselessly exercised. Hence we must embrace opportunities for humiliating ourselves, however painful they may be. As such opportunities are sent by God in His kindness and love, we must kiss the rod that strikes us, fervently utilizing the opportunity and thanking God for it.

But there is such a thing as being proud of our humility, and we may slip into that snare unawares. But if so, we are often rudely jolted out of it by some particularly painful snub or slight or the like, which shows us that we are still apt to take offense and to consider ourselves insulted, and that we are still only at the elementary stage of acquiring this virtue. For, needless to say, the saints never take offense, they never think themselves insulted, and they never complain of their treatment, or, for that matter, of anything else.

Through humility, then, as Father Augustine Baker says, we subject ourselves, our souls and bodies, with all their powers and faculties, to God's will in all things, and for His sake to all our fellows according to His will. And because God is in His creatures so for God we show humility to all others, irrespective of their merits or failings, but seeing God in them. And we also do so because He wishes us so to do, preferring others before ourselves, esteeming ourselves below them, contenting ourselves with the meanest things in food, clothes, books, and in everything else, and fleeing all honors and the esteem of mankind. And if we have this humility, then all our duties will be cheerfully and readily practiced, we will never complain for we will know that we are treated much better than we deserve, and it will therefore be impossible for us to be impatient or resentful at injuries, or unresigned in our afflictions.

This is the pathway we have to tread, especially in the religious life, and, as in other matters, we are helped along it by the fact that our Blessed Lord has trodden it before us. He has to a supreme degree shown us the way. If His divine Majesty tasted the dregs of humiliation, how can we, miserable and contemptible sinners that we are, complain if we are humbled by our fellows? "If then I, being your Lord and Master, have washed your feet, you also ought to wash one another's feet. For I have given you an example, that as I have done to you, so you do also. Amen, amen, I say to you: The servant is not greater than his lord" (John 13:14–16). But God, knowing how difficult we find this virtue and how galling it is to our nature, does not try us too sorely. Moreover, He helps us, by His own example and by His grace, to acquire humility, to crush our self-love, and to empty ourselves that He may completely possess us. For humility is a necessary preliminary if God is to possess us, and if we are to acquire other virtues. Therefore this virtue is so much stressed at the beginning of our religious life in the testing humiliations of the novitiate. But the same necessity applies throughout our lives, and we can never safely relax our vigilance in this matter. We all need to pull ourselves up sharply from time to time in this respect, and to examine carefully how we stand in regard to humility, one atom of which, according to St. Madeleine Sophie Barat, "is worth more than a mountain of good works."

What I have said concerns chiefly the practice of humility. But there is also a higher attitude possible toward this subject. St. Francis de Sales calls it "the spirit of humility," which means not merely accepting those humiliations which come to us and bearing them with resignation, but actively seeking out humiliations and experiencing them not with mere resignation but with actual joy. But on that I need not dwell now: let me simply recall it to your minds. In conclusion, consider St. Philip Neri's exhortation "to despise the whole world, to despise no member of it, to despise oneself, to despise being despised," an exhortation, by the way, which admirably illustrates the close connection pointed out at the beginning of this conference between humility and its fellow virtues of charity and fortitude. With the help of humility these two can be acquired, and they in turn will prove steppingstones to even higher things.

VII

CHARITY

A matter of the most vital importance to all of us, about which we have to be most vigilant, is the great virtue of charity. The queen of all the virtues, it is often a matter of great difficulty, for human nature tends the opposite way; but we cannot afford to neglect it, since our salvation to a great extent depends on our practice of it. It is a subject of such grave moment that we must speak openly when dealing with it.

One of the great contributions made by Christianity to man's knowledge of truth was the idea of love as a fundamental element of religion. This came as a shock to the peoples of the ancient world and seemed to them an amazing novelty. The teaching of Christ was that henceforth the keynote of religion was to be not fear (as in the pagan religions, and largely even in the Old Testament), not even adoration or thanksgiving, but love, filial familiar love. This was altogether a new conception, flowing from the fact of the fatherhood of God, by which we are not slaves or servants, but friends and even sons of God, as a result of Christ becoming man and supernaturalizing us by grace, by means of which we are brought into relations of love with our Creator.

By reason, then, of what God has done for us, the astonishing favors He has showered upon us, the primary duty and privilege of mankind is that all should love God with their whole heart, and this was to be the test of true religion. But our Blessed Lord was not content with even this. He went yet further, and made what was to the pagan mind the even more remarkable innovation of teaching that this love for God must overflow into love of our fellows, and that without exception, because it is to be based not on personal liking or even esteem, but on the relationship that we all have with God, and on His love for all. Thus Christian charity essentially has supernatural motives, and therefore we can never attain to this all-embracing charity unless we ourselves base it on supernatural motives, ignoring merely natural considerations such as personal likes or dislikes. Christian charity has nothing to do with such views. We have to see not the outside but the inside of persons, and to consider not their body or appearance or manners but their soul, which is vivified and inhabited by God and for which God died.

If the soul in the state of grace is a thing of such beauty that it draws upon itself the infinite love of God, who sees in it a reflection of His own ineffable beauty, then we, too, are logically bound to love that soul also in the same way and for the same reason. And if we truly love God, we must love whatever He loves. That is why the Savior taught that our love of God must include love of our fellow men. "If you love Me, keep My command-

ments" (John 14:15), He said; and you know that according to Him the commandments are summed up in
"Love God," and "Love your neighbor." Hence if we
love Him, we will love others; all others. For His command is not merely that we love those who love us,
even that we should also love those who are indifferent
toward us. It goes yet further and says: "Love your enemies, do good to them that hate you" (Matt. 5:44).
Such is the spirit of Christ, and to that spiritual height
Christian love must attain. Love all without exception.
Yet not only do we for the most part fail to do this, but we
often do not love even those who are not our enemies.
So far are we from obeying the difficult part of God's com-
mandment that we do not obey even the easier part.
And if this love is what Our Lord expects of even secular
people living in the world, how much more so does He
expect it of His religious, and how displeasing to Him
it must be that there should be any lack of charity in
religious houses! He said: "By this shall all men know
that you are My disciples, if you have love one for another" (John 13:35), and that was said to all Christians.
Alas, it is too often not true even of religious, who are
vowed to strive for perfection, although the command
applies to them even more strongly than it does to
others.

In his old age St. John the Evangelist was never tired
of repeating to his followers: "Little children, love one
another"; so much so, in fact, that at last they wearied of
hearing these words, and they asked him why he always

said the same thing. He replied that, if they did this, they fulfilled the whole law and that without it they did nothing. It is what we should expect from the beloved disciple, the apostle of love; and the same spirit breathes through his epistles. Gentle though he is, he has in these epistles some terrible things to say of the uncharitable. Thus we read: "Whosoever hateth his brother is a murderer" (I John 3:15). And St. James speaks of the tongue as "full of deadly poison" (Jas. 3:8), for it kills souls. On the other hand, "if any man offend not in word, the same is a perfect man" (Jas. 3:2). Elsewhere he writes: "If any man think himself to be religious, not bridling his tongue . . . this man's religion is vain" (Jas. 1:26). Consider this last thought. If we are not in charity with all, our religious life is a mockery. It is useless to multiply prayers, mortifications, and other works if we are at enmity with others. God will not hear us. He has said so. It is like trying to build the upper part of a house before we have laid firm foundations, as Scripture often declares.

You recall the Gospel text: "If therefore thou offer thy gift at the altar" (that is, offer the sacrifice of worship) "and there thou remember that thy brother hath anything against thee, leave there thy offering before the altar, and go first to be reconciled to thy brother; and then coming thou shalt offer thy gift" (Matt. 5:23 f.). These words plainly tell us that our worship is unacceptable to God so long as we are at enmity with others. And that is why without charity and self-control our life is a mockery and our good works are in vain. Does not St. Paul say precisely the same thing? "If I speak with the tongues of men and of angels, and have not charity, I am become as sounding brass or a tinkling cymbal. . . . If I should have all faith, so that I could remove mountains, and have not charity, I am nothing. And if I should distribute all my goods to feed the poor, and if I should deliver my body to be burned, and have not charity, it profiteth me nothing" (I Cor. 13:1–3). Thus charity is indispensable for the profitable performance of all good works. Since, then, charity is so necessary, we do not wonder that Christ summed it up as being the whole law. Let us take this to heart, for it is of grave moment. We must be charitable if we would be friends with God, if we would advance His interests, and if we would save our own souls.

Now, to get down to rock bottom, why are we uncharitable? Upon considering the matter, we shall find that ill will and hostility to others nearly always arise from pride or self-will (those evil growths and deadly sins which are the fundamental causes of almost all our troubles). Thus, we think we have been snubbed or insulted by someone (or we actually have been), and at once our pride is up in arms; or someone has been promoted instead of us, and again pride revolts. From this at once springs a feeling of antagonism and prejudice against that person; this feeling, if not checked, grows steadily and assumes huge proportions. It can, indeed, become an obsession, so that eventually we view everything connected with that per-

son through a mist of prejudice and we twist and distort
everything he says and does. Probably the original griev-
ance was entirely imaginary; but even if it were true and
real, that is no justification for this attitude. For how different it is from the teaching of our divine Master, who
would have us particularly love that person and cherish
the rebuff! And it is the same with self-will as a cause.
Someone has not done what we wished him to do, or has
not let us do something we wished to do. The same antagonism and prejudice arise as in the previous case, and
the spirit of uncharitableness thus grows and grows like a
cancer eating away the grace from our souls and poisoning
our religious life, as well as ruining our happiness. How
sad, how deplorable, all this is, the more so since often
such petty trifles and such unworthy feelings are the
cause!

Evidently this evil must be rooted out of us, no matter
how painful the process, and we could not make a more
profitable resolve than that of eradicating it. We have
already seen that our offering of prayer is acceptable to
God only when we are at peace with all others. Think of
that, and never forget it. Father Faber well says that the
worst kinds of unhappiness (as well as the evils described
above) come from our conduct toward each other, as well
as the greatest amount of unhappiness. For criticism,
sneers, and the like inevitably bring unhappiness to the
speaker as well as to the victim. One who says such things
is always unhappy, discontented, and secretly ashamed.
And, on the other hand, kindness, charity, gentleness

spread happiness around and give an interior happiness to him who has these qualities. Kindness has converted more people than zeal, eloquence, or learning, and these last have seldom converted anyone unless they were accompanied by kindness. Pride, as we have seen, is a fruitful cause of uncharitableness; so kindness is the easiest road to humility and to self-conquest.

How vastly different life would be for all of us if we all were invariably kind, considerate, charitable; if we never uttered the biting criticism, the clever epigram, or the sarcastic comment! What peace that would mean among all, and what peace in our own souls! And with this would necessarily go a readiness and an eagerness to forgive whatever is done or said against us; for a heart full of love cannot cherish resentment. Forgiveness is inseparably bound up with charity. And in this connection we should not forget that every time we say the Our Father we ask God to forgive us as we forgive others. That fact is often not sufficiently realized. "Forgive us our trespasses as we forgive them that trespass against us," that is, in the measure that we forgive others. Thus we condemn ourselves out of our own mouths every time we say that prayer, if we do not forgive others. The same thought is expressed by the beatitude: "Blessed are the merciful, for they shall obtain mercy" (Matt. 5:7); and also by those other texts: "In what measure you shall mete, it shall be measured to you again" (Mark 4:24); and "Judge not, that you may not be judged" (Matt. 7:1). To judge is to usurp the functions of God, who alone can judge with full justice. Let us, then, forgive, that so God may forgive us.

One of the ironies of history is that, as ancient writers tell us, the charity of the early Christians was spoken of as their leading characteristic, so that the pagans had a saying: "Behold how these Christians love one another." Now, alas, this same phrase is used with biting sarcasm by the enemies of the Church, in sneering allusion to the dissensions in Christendom, and to the individual lack of charity among the followers of Christ. But it once was true, and our Blessed Lord wished that it should always be true. He said: "By this shall all men know that you are My disciples, if you have love one for another" (John 13: 35). This bond of mutual charity was thus to be the badge of His followers. Therefore the Apostle calls charity the bond of perfection, saying: "But above all these things have charity, which is the bond of perfection" (Col. 3: 14), so that it is useless to seek perfection without it; whereas possession of charity makes up for many defects. "Charity covereth a multitude of sins" (I Pet. 4:8); so much so, indeed, that St. John says: "We know that we have passed from death to life, because we love the brethren. He that loveth not abideth in death" (I John 3:14). There you have the matter in a nutshell.

Probably most of us have in all this a subject for serious self-examination and for earnest resolutions. There we come down to the hard reality. Do we in actual fact forgive others? Have we banished from our hearts all malice, all deliberate dislike, all unkindness? Are we steadfastly resolved to refrain from criticism, often ill-informed and unjustifiable? If so, the peace of God will reign in our hearts and in the hearts of those around us, and we will make our own this beautiful prayer of St. Francis: "Lord, make me an instrument of Thy peace; where there is hatred let me sow love; where there is injury, pardon; where there is doubt, faith; where there is despair, hope; where there is darkness, light; and where there is sadness, joy. O divine Master, grant that I may not so much seek to be consoled as to console; to be understood as to understand; to be loved as to love; for it is in giving that we receive, it is in pardoning that we are pardoned, and it is in dying that we are born to eternal love." There we have a practical guide to our conduct for the future. Let us be quite resolved to lead our lives on those lines henceforth. For be sure of this: if we are not so resolved, our religious life, our sacrifices, our mortifications, our good works, are a vain delusion and a waste of effort. May God help each one of us to see into his own heart, and give us the grace bravely to conquer ourselves in this matter and to abide at all times in charity. "God is love."

VIII

THIRST FOR GOD

The title of one of Father Faber's books, *All for Jesus,* aptly sums up what must be our aim in the religious life, —with the "all" emphasized. In religion our whole being must be dedicated to God, a hard task, for we are inclined to keep something back, some little failing, or perhaps some small form of self-indulgence. But God is a jealous God (or, if you prefer it, He is a Great Lover), and He must have all. He will not share our heart with any creatures. And above all He demands this wholehearted self-dedication from His religious. Precisely because of this, there arise the uneasiness and the vague unhappiness felt by many.

Well, now, if it should happen that you are not truly happy, if light and peace seem in any degree to have deserted you, you do not need (save in exceptional cases of advanced souls) to go far to seek the cause. It is in yourself. God is calling you, attracting you, hunting you down, and you are seeking to shake Him off, because you fear that He will ask too much. Therefore you are unhappy, because you are fleeing from that alone which can give you happiness. This is the theme of that superb poem, *The Hound of Heaven,* in which Francis Thomp-

son has incomparably described how the love of God
remorselessly pursues the soul, which finds no happiness
because it is fleeing from God and His demands. Read it
again some day. Let us recall these lines:

> For, though I knew His love who followèd,
>   Yet was I sore adread
> Lest, having Him, I must have naught beside.

That is what we fear, and we often shrink from the
demands of "The Tremendous Lover," and in so doing
condemn ourselves to misery, for nothing else can satisfy
us, so that we come to realize at last the truth proclaimed
by the Voice of the Divine Hunter:

> Nigh and nigh draws the chase,
>   With unperturbèd pace,
> Deliberate speed, majestic instancy,
>   And past those noisèd Feet
>   A Voice comes yet more fleet—
> Lo! naught contents thee, who content'st not Me.

No, nothing earthly can ever satisfy the soul that has been
marked down by God as His own, and we have to learn
what is sometimes a bitter lesson. We instinctively crave
for God, but we must empty our hearts of all else if we
are to possess Him. Hence the sickness, the sorrow, and
the blindness of the world; for when God is driven out,
life is no longer worth living, since, as the same poem
sublimely ends:

> Ah, fondest,[1] blindest, weakest,
>   I am He whom thou seekest!
> Thou dravest love from thee, who dravest Me.

[1] That is, "most foolish."

Does it ever strike us sufficiently how strange it is that God should thus persistently wish for our love, and has gone so far as to implant in us a desire for Him that will not be smothered? It is amazing that He should desire us, and St. Teresa said we should thank Him for having such bad taste. But it is also surprising to us that He should give us an innate desire for Himself. Even the most worldly who neglect and ignore God all their lives have this, and it comes out on their deathbeds as a rule. For there is no real happiness without Him.

But of course this desire for God does not make itself felt if we do not give it a chance; it must be cultivated if it is to be really strong. Father Lallemant has said: "At first divine things are insipid, and it is with difficulty we can relish them; but in course of time they become sweet and so full of delicious flavour that we feel nothing but disgust for everything else. On the other hand, the things of earth which flatter the senses, are at first pleasant and delicious, but in the end we find only bitterness in them." This is profoundly true, as many of us know. Anyone who has come to the religious life after a spell in the world (a late vocation, for example) knows how distasteful much of it is at first, and what struggles the novitiate involves. But such a one also knows what sweetness he eventually finds in it, and perhaps all the more because he has had to struggle for it.

This longing for God, for holiness, for heaven on earth, is what has peopled the monasteries and convents for centuries. Do you not feel this desire? Of course you do. Even unbelievers feel it in spite of themselves; and for those who serve God in religious houses it is the motive force of their lives. And this attraction at the same time gives us confidence, for we know it comes from God; and confidence in turn makes all things easy. Confidence in God turns the steepest stairway of life into an escalator. How, then, can anyone turn his back on this drawing to God, or turn deaf ears to His call? How can anyone be indifferent to God or to religion, which is simply the service of God? It is because he has not given it a chance. The first step is the hardest, like the first plunge into the water when bathing, or like mortification, of which St. John Vianney said it was only the first step that was hard. "Spiritual delights," we are told by Father James, the Capuchin, "have no appeal except for those who have some experience of them. Once possessed, they remove the thirst for other things."

Thirst: that is the word. It was often used by our Lord. "If any man thirst, let him come to Me and drink" (John 7:37); and again: "He that shall drink of the water that I will give him shall not thirst forever" (John 4:13), that is, he shall be satiated. Nothing else, indeed, can satiate us. God is a perennial fountain of life and grace within us. This is the work of the Holy Ghost; it is the reason why Christ left the earth, that so God might be really present and operating in each of us by the Holy Spirit. St. Paul declares: "The charity of God is poured forth in our hearts, by the Holy Ghost who is given to us" (Rom. 5:5). Yes, the Holy Ghost is ceaselessly working in the souls of those who are in grace; by Him our souls live and move and have their being, so that this present life becomes a foretaste of heaven, and every moment brings its encouragement and its increase of love.

Now, if God thus wishes to draw us to Him, it is for our own good. Over and over again He says in the New Testament that He longs to give us peace and happiness, and in tender imagery He declares: "How often would I have gathered thy children as the bird doth her brood under her wings, and thou wouldest not?" (Luke 13: 34.) No, they would not let Him, for they did not understand wherein lay their welfare and happiness. Well might He lament, as He wept over Jerusalem: "If thou also hadst known, and that in this thy day, the things that are to thy peace: but now they are hidden from thy eyes" (Luke 19:42). For this peace and happiness are not what the world understands by those words. The peace that He gives thrives upon suffering and persecution, whereas the world fancies these are destructive of peace. But He Himself declares: "My peace I give unto you: not as the world giveth, do I give unto you" (John 14:27); that is, His peace is of another kind, independent of all disturbances and trials, and unshaken by them. And when His followers realized this and experienced the peace and happiness that come from suffering for Him, then would His prophecy be fulfilled: "Your sorrow shall be turned into joy. . . . And your joy no man shall take from you" (John 16:20, 22).

God, then, wishes to give us joy,[2] but only if we obey His call and if we follow the path he has marked out for us. He has told us that He is the way, the truth, and the life. Moreover He has said: "I am the light of the world. He that followeth Me walketh not in darkness, but shall have the light of life" (John 8:12). The following of Christ, then, is the way of peace and light and happiness.

But of course our free will can oppose itself to following this path, and it often does so. What fools we are! We turn from the reality to the shadows, from the one essential, to childish toys, though we know that only dissatisfaction and unhappiness can result from such a course. Listen to St. Augustine: "Placed as it is between God and creatures, the human soul by turning to its Creator is enlightened, ennobled, and perfected; by turning to creatures it is blinded, degraded, and corrupted." Scripture, for its part, expresses it thus: "Seek ye therefore first the kingdom of God and His justice; and all these things shall be added unto you" (Matt. 6: 33), that is, if you completely possess God, you will not desire anything else, for you will have everything. Hence the Easter liturgy repeats time and again the admonition: "Mind the things that are above, not the things that are upon the earth" (Col. 3:2). And St. Paul adds the reason, which is specially applicable to religious: "For you are dead; and your life is hid with Christ in God" (Col. 3:3).

[2] Cf. John 15:11 (Knox's trans.: "All this I have told you, so that my joy may be yours, and the measure of your joy may be filled up."

Do we realize that sufficiently? Are we dead to the world? Immediately after taking the vows, the religious lies on a pall or under one, surrounded by funeral candles, symbolizing thereby his death to the world; and when we lie there we, each of us, generously determined that henceforth we would be in truth dead to the world. But have we become so? If we were, we would live entirely in and for Christ, and with St. Paul we could say: "I live, now not I; but Christ liveth in me" (Gal. 2:20); and again with the same Apostle: "For to me, to live is Christ; and to die is gain" (Phil. 1:21).

That is what God expects of us; He warns us that we cannot serve both Him and mammon, that is, the world. And not only that, but we must hate the latter, and take up our cross daily and follow Him. The religious life faithfully led is a daily taking up of the cross. This is a hard saying, but after all it was to do this that we entered the religious life. We came to do not our own will but the will of God; in fact, one of the main objects of a religious house is to provide a place wherein those dwelling in it will have the safeguard of not being able to do their own will. And the giving up of our will is the hardest thing and the greatest sacrifice of all, so that St. Gregory says: "It is a little thing to give up what we have, but it is a very great thing to give up what we are." That we do by relinquishing our own will. We are thereby no longer our own, but are the slaves of God.

Do you recall how St. Bernard used to ask himself daily: "Bernard, why art thou come hither?" This he did to rekindle his fervor and to hearten him in the struggle against himself, that struggle which we all must wage and which has as its end the annihilation of self-will. A holy religious when asked what he did during his novitiate, replied: "There were two of us. I had to pick up one and pitch him out the window." Yes, there are two of us in each of us, and the warfare must be waged. Hence the great value of the life, and the fact that it has been called a daily martyrdom if fully and faithfully led.

It is all the more a martyrdom if, as often happens, God seems to leave us to fight our warfare alone, to withdraw Himself far from us and thereby to deprive us of all light and consolation. This is a terrible trial for the soul, yet it is most salutary, as it makes us see we have no grounds for hope in ourselves or in our works, and leads us to realize more clearly our need of God. It is, in fact, often to increase our thirst for God that He sends us this sense of abondonment. He would not have us find help in ourselves or in our good works; indeed, He cannot tolerate that in souls seeking perfection, for it is both the result and the cause of self-love and pride. Hence He strips us of that by making us pass through dereliction and spiritual desolation. Only when we are tried in the fires of suffering, when we have been reduced to nothingness, can He make full use of us, and can we be useful instruments in His hand. This fact, also, Francis Thompson has well expressed when he wrote:

Ah! must—
Designer infinite!—
Ah! must Thou char the wood ere Thou canst limm with it?

The wood has to be reduced to charcoal before the Great
Artist can make use of it to trace His designs. Hence,
in His infinite wisdom, He deprives us of all resources
and of all trust in ourselves; and then, indeed, is the soul
in darkness, and, not understanding God's plan, it cries
out in agony because all seems to be lost. Yet in reality the
opposite is the truth, for all is not lost, but gained. Hear
once again the poet putting the words into God's mouth:

All which I took from thee I did but take,
  Not for thy harms,
But just that thou might'st seek it in My arms.
All which thy child's mistake
Fancies as lost, I have stored for thee at home:
Rise, clasp My hand, and come.

But the soul in this condition does not realize all that. It
is like the apostles tossed in the storm upon the lake, amid
darkness and threatening waves. But eventually, like
them, when things seem at their worst, the soul hears the
voice of the Beloved: "Peace, be not afraid, it is I"; and
there follows a great calm. By this means the soul receives
that holy hope so well known to the saints, a hope based
solely on God, the last traces of trust in ourselves having
been destroyed.

"This saying is hard; and who can hear it?" (John
6:61.) We may well re-echo that cry of the Jews around
Our Lord. But bear in mind that Christ says: "You have

not chosen Me, but I have chosen you" (John 15:16). We owe our vocation to Him, and therefore we have a claim on His support, a fact that gives us great encouragement. He has selected us, and for this particular house. He has gathered this community together, sending each one hither. He has meant us to have these particular companions, and no other. In the same way He has given us a work to do which none other can do, for He wishes it done by us. Each of us fills a special niche in His plan. We must not foil this plan by faintheartedness or failure to correspond to the graces which God gives us. He knows full well our weakness and frailty and He makes every allowance. The Psalmist beautifully says: "As far as the east is from the west, so far hath He removed our iniquities from us. As a father hath compassion on his children, so hath the Lord compassion on them that fear Him. For He knoweth our frame. He remembereth that we are dust" (Ps. 102:12–14). The grace of God makes possible for us whatever God asks of us, and it is a theological axiom that "to him who does his best, God does not deny grace."

But we must persist in our efforts to advance in virtue. "He that perseveres to the end, he shall be saved." In religion no standing still is possible. It is like a slippery slope; if we halt, we slip back. We can never rest satisfied, but must continue laboring to advance along the road that winds uphill to the end. Self-satisfaction is suicide; we must never be satisfied with our condition. "He that thinketh himself to stand, let him take heed lest he fall" (I Cor.

10:12). Therefore we must continue to strive, at the same time putting all our trust in God and leaving the result to Him.

Here again we must calmly accept God's will, practicing abandonment to God not only in the trials of life, but also as regards the success or apparent failure of our labors, even our labors for our own perfection. The great St. Teresa declared: "I ask only so much perfection and interior life as it shall please God to give me, and that only at the time He has ordained." We must always strive, but we must strive peacefully, leaving the result contentedly to God. Never, then, should we be unduly perturbed by our falls. Such defeats are allowed by God, just as our weakness is sent to us that it may become our victorious battleground. Our defeats can help us enormously by schooling us in humility and patience, and such defeats can be immensely more useful than victories which are spoilt by vain complacency.

Never be unduly distressed when things seem dark around you or your affairs all seem to go wrong. In fact, do not be distressed at all at any time. God is but hiding Himself temporarily from you in order to draw you nearer to Him, to make you realize your dependence on Him, and to increase your thirst for Him. Though He may not make His presence known, yet He is with you, and in His own good time He will whisper: "Peace I leave with you; My peace I give unto you. Not as the world giveth, do I give unto you" (John 14:27). This peace is the pearl of great price for the acquisition of which no payment is too great, and for the sake of which the world is well lost to us. Without it nothing pleases us, without complete surrender to God nothing brings happiness, without wholehearted service given to Him nothing satisfies us.

"Lo! naught contents thee, who contentest not Me." But the faithful servant of Christ has an abounding peace no matter what cares, what trials, what pains God in His goodness and wisdom sends. Such things but draw such a one closer to God, in whom alone is the joy that the world cannot give, and in whom we find the hundredfold reward promised to us in this life and the yet greater reward in the life to come.

IX

MORTIFICATION

Not the least of the many paradoxes of Christianity is that afflictions, whether of soul or body, can cause great joy; indeed so much is this the case that a mortified, austere community is always a happy one. This truth also helps to explain the fact that the saints have a thirst for mortification. But when we reflect on the matter, we find that this is not so strange as it might at first sight seem. Perhaps the chief reason is the fact that only by cutting off self-indulgence, by "dying to ourselves," can we remove the obstacles that stand between us and God, so that only by this means can we make possible that close union with God which is the primary aim of the religious life and which in itself brings bliss to the soul. If we live only for God, without self-seeking and without concessions to self, we are, in the nature of things, bound to be happy. And further reason for this joy arising from mortification is that we know we are thereby, in St. Paul's striking phrase, filling up "those things that are wanting of the sufferings of Christ" (Col. 1:24), doing our share in supplying that measure of suffering which God expects from His mystical body. Thus our pains and trials, being united to the sacred sufferings of Christ, have a definite redemptive value, giving us thus a share in the redemptive work of our Savior. In brief, then, it may be said that the joy conferred by practicing mortification comes from the sweetness of God's yoke, and by the knowledge that by these pains we are, through the merits of Christ, freeing our own souls and those of others from sin and from the punishments due to sin, as well as atoning to God for those sins. Thus on all these counts we gladden the heart of God and the angels.

Mortification, then, plays an important and a happy part in our life. Indeed, whether it be spiritual or bodily or both, it is needful for the leading of a holy life. Moreover, it cannot harm us if it is moderate, discreet, and sanctioned by our superiors. This last condition is important, for, as St. Benedict strongly insists in his Rule, we must have permission for our external mortifications, since otherwise they are liable to be merely the fruit of self-will and pride, and will be looked upon by God as presumption, so that they can produce no good. Now mortification is sacrifice, and Christianity is founded on sacrifice: our Blessed Lord's on the cross, and that of each of His true followers every day. It is, therefore, needful, and Jesus, speaking to the crowd surrounding Him, expressed this bluntly and tersely when He declared: "If any man come to Me, and hate not his father and mother and wife and children and brethren and sisters, yea and his own life also, he cannot be My disciple" (Luke 14:26). This is a way of saying that a man must esteem them as nothing when compared with Christ.

Again He said: "If any man will come after Me, let him deny himself and take up his cross daily and follow Me" (Luke 9:23). Thus God must come first in our lives, and no attachments, whether to persons or to things, can be allowed in our hearts. Everything else must be sacrificed for Him, because nothing can be permitted to stand between us and Him, or to steal away part of that love which is all due to Him. That is Christian self-denial (and the reason for it) in a nut shell. God first, last, and all the time, and other things only for Him.

There we have the "royal road of the cross"; mortifications are sharp swords that will sever the bonds holding us back from God. "The cords of the wicked have encompassed me," cries the Psalmist; "but I have not forgotten Thy law" (Ps. 118:61), the law of self-denial which will free us. One of Father Bernard Vaughan's pithy sayings was: "We must win our crowns, not woo them," that is, win them by suffering. He added that, if we would follow the higher and fuller life of perfection, as every religious must, the cross is necessary for us: "You must follow Our Lord through the passion-tide of a religious noviciate, press on to Calvary and be contented, with Him, to be nailed to the cross by the three vows of poverty, chastity, and obedience. Then, dead to this world, you shall rise to a new life, to a life glorious indeed, because to it Our Lord has promised a hundredfold on earth, and eternal happiness in heaven."

In the cross, then, must be all our joy, however much our lower nature may shudder. The more it shudders, the more our spirit rejoices. This is so with each of us, and therefore this battle between grace and nature, between spirit and flesh, has necessarily to be waged by us all; for it cannot be shirked, and much hangs on the result. The cross is the source of truest joy; and therefore the sign of the cross has always been beloved by Catholics.

> Whene'er across this sinful flesh of mine
> I draw the holy sign,
> All good thoughts stir within me, and renew
> Their slumbering strength divine;
> Till there springs up a courage high and true
> To suffer and to do.[1]

And then we can cry out with the Psalmist: "I am ready, and am not troubled" (Ps. 118:60). For courage and generosity grow with the practice of them.

So we must carefully consider what holds us back from God, and from giving ourselves wholeheartedly, and, if we find anything, anything to which we have too great an attachment, we must generously cast it from us. "If thy right eye scandalize thee" (if it is an occasion of sin to you), "pluck it out" (Matt. 5:29). If there is anything that is to us an occasion of venial sin, we must boldly cut it off, for it cannot come from God and it impedes our union with Him. Yet all this sternness with ourselves is not a cause of sadness but rather of joy. We have already seen some of the reasons why mortification causes joy in us, and that is what God desires: He does not wish us to be unhappy, but full of joy and peace, and those things

---

[1] Cardinal Newman.

are to be found in the practice of penance, in which we are tremendously helped by grace, so that St. Augustine could say that he had thought self-control to be impossible until he had felt the power of grace. Thus, helped by God and especially encouraged by the example we have in the sufferings of our divine Lord, who, "having joy set before Him, endured the cross" (Heb. 12:2), we are given courage to walk in the path of self-denial. Thus we come to the systematic doing of what we do not wish to do, simply because we do not wish to do it, both as penance for sin and as a mode of self-discipline: the "*agere contra*" of the Jesuits, in fact, which principle Father Doyle was so fond of. And in this connection we may recall that one of his favorite mortifications was that of forcing himself to do every small duty with his whole heart—what he called "the constant mortification of intense fervor at each little duty." That may sound little, but it involves a very great deal.

We can never afford to forget that we are members of the mystical body of Christ, and as such we must be crucified, for God wills that the members of His body should suffer with its Head and thereby continue through all time the redemptive work begun on Calvary. And incidentally this fact is the key to much of the enigma of life with its sore trials, its pains and disappointments. The average man is quite ignorant of the real significance of suffering, let alone its value; indeed he can see no purpose in it at all. How different, then, his attitude from that of St. Augustine's famous, "Domine, hic ure, his seca, hic non parcas,

ut in aeternum parcas," or St. Teresa's, "Aut pati, aut
mori." If mankind could but faintly grasp the value of
suffering, the world would be a very different place.

There are, then, many reasons why mortification is necessary. A further important consideration is that our facility in prayer largely depends on it, since without some
kind of systematic self-denial we cannot pray well. And
why? Because we cannot have close union with God unless we fulfill the conditions laid down by Himself, and
one of these was that we should take up our cross daily.
But another reason for it is that self-indulgence is the
enemy of fervor, and it also fills the mind with distracting
images, and the heart with counter-attractions, both of
which prevent prayer. Indeed, so true is this connection
between mortification and prayer that one spiritual master has roundly declared: "There is a definite connection
between how we take our food and how we pray." We
know, too, that mortification has the effect of producing
peace of mind, largely because it strengthens the power
of the will over the passions. That is one of several reasons
why the most mortified individuals or communities are
usually the most contented and cheerful, whereas the self-
indulgent are generally restless and unhappy. A further
reason for this truth we see in the fact that mortification is
the outward expression of love, for as Newman said: "Self-
denial is the measure of love." After all, people in the
world voluntarily suffer many things for purely worldly
motives (chiefly from vanity, self-love), as, for instance,
living a life of very hard work for the sake of accumulating

riches or fame; and women suffer tortures and endless deprivations for the sake of their appearance: fasting so as to be slim, wearing tight shoes, and the like. If they can so act from an unworthy motive, surely we can be equally courageous in view of the wonderful motive and reward that we have. The *Imitation of Christ* tells us that we should love to suffer for Christ, and we know that St. Paul taught precisely the same lesson, using as his illustration the self-denial practiced by athletes training for a race; "they, indeed, that they may receive a corruptible crown, but we an incorruptible one" (I Cor. 9:25).

It is strange that the modern world for the most part fails to understand the necessity of mortification. There is a craze for self-indulgence. Yet we all have secretly a prompting to mortify ourselves, if we do not utterly stifle it. Shirking this merely causes unhappiness, because of the feeling of slackness which this produces, and because of consequent sins. Needless to say, all this specially applies to religious, to whom St. John Damascene wrote: "You who are religious, if you desire to be united to Jesus crucified, should present yourself to Jesus as crucified or willing to be crucified"; and St. Joseph Calasanctius declared: "A day passed without mortification is a day lost."

And now to consider how to put all this doctrine into practice. Mortifications are either external or internal, either bodily or spiritual; and it may be stressed at once that, except in those orders that were specially founded for the practice of bodily mortification, such as the Carmelites and the Poor Clares, there is as a rule little need or

scope for bodily mortification; it is, in fact, often unde-
sirable. In most cases the ordinary life of the house is quite
hard enough, and moreover our health and our consequent ability to perform the duties expected of us must be
considered. In any event, as already stated, it is necessary
that the leave of the superior be first obtained for any extraordinary penances. Internal spiritual mortifications are
much better; they are not showy, and therefore they afford
no scope for pride or display or singularity; they are not
harmful to the health; and they can be practiced at all
times of the day without interfering with our work. It is
obvious that these are particularly suitable for an active
religious, and that such a one should not practice mortification in food to any great extent over and above what the
Rule demands, or as regards sleep, prayers, and watching.

But, on the other hand, there is never any need to restrain our internal mortifications. The more of them the
better, and they can be of all sorts. St. Alphonsus advises
us that "the best, most useful, and least dangerous mortifications are the neglected ones by which we abstain from
things lawful, and for which we need no permissions; for
instance, not to yield to curiosity in seeing or hearing
something, to speak little, to be satisfied with less palata-
ble or poor food, to rejoice if necessary things are wanting
to us, not to complain of the weather, suffering, or sickness, of contempt or persecution." Especially we should
seek to check impetuosity. For instance, it is an excellent
thing to refrain from opening a letter for several hours
after receiving it, to refrain from trying to have our par-

ticular work changed, or from novelties of all kinds. Not only are such acts of self-restraint mortifications, but they also induce calmness, and calmness contributes to strength. Another class of mortifications is most useful, and comes under the heading of kindness to others: for example, charity, helping the sick, the aged, or the sorrowful at personal inconvenience to ourselves. Such deeds give us mortification for ourselves, exercise the virtue of charity, and afford positive help to others.

Then, in a variety of ways, there is mortification of the intellect, which is specially useful because intellectual pride is such a deadly danger. Thus we can restrain our curiosity for news, and we can submit our opinion to that of others. A good religious never stubbornly maintains his own views. We can mortify ourselves by never arguing or insisting on our point of view. Different persons have different views, but the mortification consists in submitting our judgment for God's sake to that of others, even our equals or inferiors, but still more so, of course, to superiors. St. Robert Bellarmine says: "Far better an ounce of charity than a hundred cart-loads of reason." Therefore give way and do not argue. Have a contest as to who will give way first, or as St. Paul puts it: "In honor preventing one another," that is, forestalling one another. But perhaps the best mortification of all (and it can be a very real one) is the meticulous keeping of the Rule even in the smallest details. This practice gives endless opportunities for penance and self-restraint, and is, of course, a virtue in itself as well.

Well, there we have many practices of mortification which anyone can use and which are an excellent discipline, and you can doubtless think of many others. But they are of little or no use if they are only isolated incidents in our lives, and only occasionally performed. We need to form a habit, because our object is the strengthening of the will (as distinct from the object of penance, which is an atoning for sin); and so we require a habit. Therefore we must act up to Our Lord's injunction about taking up the cross daily. God will give us the grace to do so, if we, for our part, have courage and determination, and above all if we are animated by a love of Him.

X

DEATH

There is no Catholic who does not know that the whole object of this life is to prepare us for the next life. The Catechism reminds us that the object of our creation is to qualify us for eternal life, and therefore everything else in life is secondary to that main object. Yet how little this simple though tremendously important fact is realized! Millions of people live only for this life, they direct their efforts and ambitions only to the things of this world (wealth, health, happiness, success, pleasure, luxury), and they completely ignore the real object of life, the only thing that greatly matters. In other words, they make the means into an end and are thereby grievously deceived. What folly and tragic blindness this is!

But we religious do not need reminding that the next life is what counts, that this life on earth is but a trifle, and a quickly fleeting one at that, and that the sensible Christian will see things in their right proportion. Because we realize all that, we are here in a religious house. We know well that we are in this world for but a very short time, and that then comes eternity. We know that we are like actors playing a brief part on the stage. As a player emerges from the wings of a theater on one side and for a brief space holds the center of the stage before passing out through the wings on the other side, so we have behind us the untold ages of the past centuries, and we have at our disposal the brief span of years that may be allotted to us during which to hold the stage, before we, too, pass out through the wings on the other side into the realms of eternity. That being so, the "realities" of this present life pale into insignificance before the great realities of everlasting life beyond the grave. It is, then, the next life that matters, and therefore everything in this present life must be made subordinate to that supreme end if we would be truly wise; and all our actions must be dominated by that governing principle. "Eternity! Eternity!" We can understand why many a monastic cell has those significant words prominently displayed; for those words tell everything, and in face of them everything else dwindles and withers to its true insignificance.

But if the thought of eternity thus teaches us to see life in its true light, it also teaches us to view death in its proper perspective; and that is equally important. For in what a foolish and mistaken manner many people look at death, when they can be induced to think of it at all! The vast majority prefer to ignore it, to forget it, and, like the ostrich sticking its head into the sand when pursued, they try to persuade themselves that it does not exists, or at least that it is so far off that it does not now matter. And all the time it is inexorably drawing nearer. Since every day brings it nearer, it is true that we were never nearer death than at this moment. And within what is, comparatively speaking, only a few days each one of us, no matter to what age we should live, will have passed out of this life on earth.

But what of it? Surely to the Christian that must be a cause for great rejoicing, since the nearer we are to the happy moment of our release and to the beginning of our real life the more reason there is for joy; at any rate for us religious, if we have devoted our lives to serving God and thereby preparing for death. If life is not a preparation for death, it is a tragic farce. For death is the great interpreter of life. It, and what follows it, alone give a meaning to life. But for the next life, and the explanation which it affords of our life on earth, this life would be but a meaningless enigma.

Therefore it is irrational to fear death unduly, to cling desperately to the hope of life, and still more so to center all our actions and plans on this life alone. Only after death do we really begin to live. Death is the gateway into life, the real life, and only when we have passed through that gateway do we begin to fulfill the real object of our creation when we take our places in the eternal courts and raise our voices amid the angelic choirs in the eternal hymn: "Holy, Holy, Holy." Thus our faith leads us to look forward ardently to death, while we are at the same time willing to continue to labor in what the *Salve Regina* terms "this vale of tears" for as long as it shall please God. This is precisely the attitude shown by St. Martin of Tours, of whom the Breviary tells us that, when he lay dying and rejoicing in the fact, his monks (of whom he was abbot) besought him not to leave them desolate and fatherless. Whereupon, though he wished to die, he cried out to God: "If Thou dost wish me yet to labor longer, I do not refuse." That is the attitude we should all have: the faithful laborer, eager for his rest, longing to meet his Creator, yet still ready to work and to suffer further for his Lord.

Someone has said that no subject is so teeming with platitudes as death. Yet those very platitudes are of the utmost importance (as, indeed, are many platitudes), and St. Paul expressed the most vital of them when he declared that death was not an ending but a birth, the birth of real life. This is why the moment of death is the most important moment of life: for it is the starting-point of our eternity, the crucial moment of our existence. It is the end of the dangers and mischances of life, so that even the pagan Aristotle could say: "Call no man happy until he is dead." This being so, death must be anticipated, prepared for, more than any other moment; and, in fact, we are preparing for it, either well or badly, every minute of our lives. For everything that we willfully do or refrain from doing has a good or a bad effect on our position in eternity. When the well-known Dominican, Father Bertrand Wilberforce, lay dying, he was asked if he were not afraid to die. His trenchant reply was: "Do you think I am such a fool as to be afraid of that for which I have been preparing all my life?"

To the supernatural man death is not an evil, nor yet a foe, but a friend, and a welcome friend.

"Dear beauteous death, the jewel of the just," is how it is described by Henry Vaughan, the Stuart poet. How should we consider it otherwise when we realize that it is an end only of present paltry deceitful joys, of present sorrows and dangers and troubles; while it is the beginning of a bliss beyond our comprehension or our imagination? "Eye hath not seen nor ear heard . . . what things God hath prepared for them that love Him" (I Cor. 2:9). Therefore death is a happiness to those who have tried hard to lead a good life, to those also who have at times not led a good life but who have repented and done penance (perhaps even more so for them), and to those who have lived not for self but for God and for their fellow creatures, the otherworldly, in fact, who have lived with the next world always in view.

Yes, that is the whole point: the making of this life a preparation for death. I have already said that everything we think, say, or do is, in fact, a preparation, good or bad, for death; but Father Faber in one of his conferences gives certain useful details regarding that preparation. "A life of general preparation for death," he says, "is a life that has avoided these seven things: lukewarmness, careless sacraments, waste of time, worldliness, changeableness in devotions, selfish scantiness of almsgiving, and want of penance. These are the seven prophecies of unquiet and distressing deaths." Let us take to heart, then, the advice of St. Angela of Merici: "Never do anything you would have wished not to have done if you died to-night." We must be always ready for the call ("Blessed is the man whom when the Lord cometh He shall find watching"), for if there is one thing as sure as the certainty of our death it is the uncertainty of the time of its coming. "The day of the Lord shall so come as a thief in the night" (I Thess. 5:2). How often we have sad and striking instances of that! The loving hand of God reaches out and gathers in one who seemed to have yet many years of labor ahead; and so, too, it may be with any of us. Therefore we must always be prepared, even as St. Paul told Timothy that he was ready. Recall his words: "For I am even now ready to be sacrificed; and the time of my dissolution is at hand" (II Tim. 4: 6). To be sacrificed. Death is the last and best act of self-sacrifice, the final act of abnegation. As religious, let our daily acts of self-sacrifice be a preparation for the supreme act of sacrifice, death.

And after death? Then comes the supreme moment of the particular judgment. The soul has been conducted by the angels to the throne of God. The imagination fails us at this point; but read Newman's *Dream of Gerontius,* if you have not already done so. It is unforgettable. Then, at that moment after death, we shall hear our sentence and know that we shall receive our reward, "the crown that is laid up for them that love His coming," as St. Paul assures us. So long as we have been in the state of grace we have been accumulating merits, though we must not forget the other side of the matter: the debt for past sins still to be paid, our infidelities to grace, our negligences, and we must try to pay that debt before death comes, by penance, by accepting what sufferings God sends in this life, and by the gaining of indulgences. St. Paul says that the crown is not only for himself but for all who love Christ's coming. Love His coming in Holy Communion, love His coming in the guise of a cross or in the persons of the poor or the sick, love the thought of His coming at the moment of death, and above all love His holy will. "Be thou faithful unto death," He says to us, "and I will give thee the crown of life" (Apoc. 2:10).

That reward is already awaiting us, it has already been prepared for us, and we have the assurance that "the sufferings of this time are not worthy to be compared with the glory to come that shall be revealed in us" (Rom. 8:18). Therefore at times we should encourage ourselves with the glad reflection that soon we shall all be face to face with God. In view of that, what else matters? We are within sight of the end, all of us, irrespective of age, and therefore within sight of the beginning for which we were made. Soon we shall hear that tender voice saying: "Come, ye blessed of My Father, possess you the kingdom prepared for you" (Matt. 25: 34). That is what we are waiting for, that is what we long to hear. For we are beings made for God, destined to be with God forever. Birth, life, and death are but episodes, dwarfed to nothing in this grand eternal plan. Hence we are unreasonable when we grieve unduly over the death of a near relation or friend. But we are not as the heathen, without hope. For them death means the

end of everything, and so their grief and despair at the
death of a loved one is understandable. But we know
that the fact is very different; we know that the loved
one is to be envied as having left behind the pains and
sorrows of this world, as having passed into the real life
beyond, and as having thus progressed a stage nearer to
God. So far as the deceased one, therefore, is concerned,
we can but rejoice. There thus remains as cause for grief
only our own sense of loss, which must be swallowed up
to a great extent surely by our supernatural outlook, by
our realization that for the deceased it is pure gain and
that for ourselves it is also gain since God wills that we
should no longer have the bodily company of that person,
and consequently that the death in question is the best
thing that could happen. All this is plain common sense,
but in such circumstances we are generally overcome by
our feelings at the expense of our reason. A reasonable degree of sorrow is natural and right (Our Lord Himself
groaned and wept at the death of His friend Lazarus),
but excessive paroxysms of grief and unduly prolonged
sorrow are not only unreasonable and harmful, but can be
sinful, as showing the absence of a spiritual outlook on
the matter and lack of acquiescence in the will of God.
In this matter above all others our faith, our religion,
makes a great difference, and is our consolation and
strength. Without this underlying faith all the meaning
of this life caves in and falls to pieces. With it, life and
death are one, and both are absorbed in victory.

XI

TRIBULATIONS

The laity in the world often imagine that those who live in convents or monasteries enjoy a life of unbroken fervor and union with God, free from all troubles and from spiritual anxieties. We should not be surprised at their mistaken notion. It is true that God gives us great graces, and it is true that our spiritual progress is thus made much easier. But that is only one side of the picture. For those whom God especially loves, and for whom He has special designs, He tries in the fire of tribulations, and He has always acted thus. For the dross must be burnt out of us, self-love must be killed, and opportunities for meriting greater graces must be given, and all this necessitates the experiencing of many trials. There is no need to enlarge on these truths; we all know them, at least by repute, and most of us have actual and prolonged experience of them. It is enough to say that they are of two main kinds: external, which may consist of petty but persisting annoyances, or else of really great difficulties or even physical pains or infirmities; and internal, consisting of spiritual dryness or desolation and the like.

But we cannot be astonished by this. In fact, we are warned by the experience of our predecessors and by

Holy Writ itself that this is inevitable. St. Paul told the Hebrews: "Whom the Lord loveth, He chastiseth; and He scourgeth every son whom He receiveth" (Heb. 12:6). Our divine Lord Himself gives us the reason: "Every one that beareth fruit, He will purge [prune] it that it may bring forth more fruit" (John 15:2). Only by such treatment can we be prepared to become of some use to God, for without preliminary suffering there is normally no progress in holiness, and without holiness we cannot hope to bear fruit in our labors for God. Life starts with pain and it ends with pain, and the religious life starts with the purifying tribulations of the novitiate and may well continue with tribulations of diverse kinds to the very end, for St. Paul teaches that "through many tribulations we must enter into the kingdom of God" (Acts 14:21).

Yet underneath all this suffering and pervading it all is real joy, and that not in spite of the tribulations but by reason of them. For we know that they are sent by God, that they are therefore His will, and that consequently they must be good for us. We also realize that they are the necessary preliminaries to holiness, and the sign of God's love for us. Furthermore we know that they will be followed by the glory of eternal bliss. We have already seen in a previous chapter how voluntary mortifications cause joy, and the same applies to the type of tribulations that we are now considering, and for the same reasons.

Hence the Apostle could tell the Romans: "We glory also in tribulation, knowing that tribulation worketh patience" (Rom. 5:3), that is, patience, endurance, is a

great gift; it sweetens everything. And, since it is conferred by tribulation (if that tribulation is freely accepted), the great Apostle asks almost scornfully: "Who
then shall separate us from the love of Christ? Shall tribulation?" (Rom. 8:35.) Let us see to it, then, that by a right
use of tribulations we are not separated from Christ (for
instance, by peevishness, impatience, faintheartedness),
but on the contrary are strengthened by those very tribulations in our love of Christ.

Thus St. Paul pours out comfort and consolation to the
sorely tried early Christians, and all his words are applicable to us today, because the same motives and principles
are still at work and are still valid: a fact that has always
upheld religious in their trials. But "forewarned is forearmed," and we need at times to remind ourselves to expect tribulations. Hence we read: "Son, when thou comest
to the service of God . . . prepare thy soul for temptation" (Ecclus. 2:1): words that might well be framed on
the wall of every novice's cell. Not only do they forearm
us, but they also dispel the harmful and false ultra-
romantic ideas of convent life with a cold douche of
realism.

For these reasons, then, the religious life is studded
with difficulties, and for these reasons those difficulties
are pleasant and welcomed. It is all summed up by St.
Peter thus: "Now you must be for a little time made sorrowful in divers temptations, that the trial of your faith
(much more precious than gold which is tried by the fire)
may be found unto praise and glory and honor at the ap-

pearing of Jesus Christ" (I Pet. 1:6 f.). Although with the Psalmist the religious can truthfully cry: "For Thy sake we are killed all the day long: we are counted as sheep for the slaughter" (Ps. 43:22); yet also he holds his head up and continues joyfully his journey toward God, saying confidently: "If God be for us, who is against us?" (Rom. 8:31.)

You see, then, that we have great grounds for courage, confidence, and joy in the religious life. "Who is like unto God?" And He is fighting on our side and wishes our salvation. Therefore we have no grounds for depression, still less for sadness or discouragement. Those spring from the devil and do his work, and they cause immense harm to souls. Always, then, be optimistic, though not foolishly so. After all, we have the most potent of allies. Discouragement comes from originally rating ourselves too highly, and over-estimating our abilities. We should remember that frequent small failings do not indicate that we are not progressing. On the contrary, we progress by means of them. We are aiming at the highest thing attainable in this life (perfection, or union with God), and so we must expect to fail sometimes. Moreover we can do nothing ourselves except be of good will and take care to correspond faithfully with the grace which God sends us.

It may also help us in our struggle if we bear in mind that perfection is a relative matter. We are perfect in so far as we correspond with the degree of grace that is given to us. A saint fully makes use of the grace he receives. But we do not all receive the same amount, and thus perfection does not mean the same standard for all. God does not intend that we should all reach the same level: "In My Father's house there are many mansions" (John 14:2). Thus one who has reached a lower degree of union and self-conquest may well be nearer perfection than one who has reached a higher stage but has received greater grace, because the former may have corresponded more fully than the latter with the grace received. From all this, then, it follows that we cannot judge our progress by the presence or absence of faults; nor, for that matter, does God wish us to be able to estimate our progress, for that might well be most harmful and dangerous for us.

In any case there can be no sure progress without failure; and the very fact that our failures cause us dissatisfaction shows our good will; if the will is firmly directed to God, all is well. Depression is selfishness, for it springs from undue preoccupation with ourselves; whereas cheerfulness, especially under failure, is true selflessness and meritorious, so long as it is not mere thoughtlessness and indifference. We should realize, too, that failure in the eyes of the world is often success in God's eyes, even though it may also seem to be failure in our own eyes. In any event true wisdom admonishes us, if we have made sincere and earnest efforts, to accept our failures of any sort (not only spiritual failures), as permitted by God. What God requires of us is that we should do our best, not necessarily that we should succeed. If we do our best, the good fruits will come in God's good time.

If we always act thus, we shall ever have the Holy Ghost

with us, He who is the expression of the love of God, who fills us with grace, who enlightens and guides us, who fills us with happiness, who bestows on us the theological virtues of faith, hope, and charity, and the cardinal virtues of justice, prudence, fortitude, and temperance, He who, in short, is the animating principle of the Church, and is both light and warmth to us. The Holy Ghost transforms us by divine grace, uniting us to God, placing us in special relations with God. The gift of the Holy Ghost makes a vast difference between the Christian and the non-Christian. It is He who gives us a relish for holy things, a relish that is lost by sin; it is He who gives us the desire to please God, the joy we find in loving Him, the determination we have to be faithful to Him. Is it any wonder, then, that our Blessed Lord said it was expedient for us that He should go that the Paraclete might come to us? He, the Sanctifier, has been justly called the Forgotten Paraclete. For how often we forget Him! How few have a real devotion to the Holy Ghost, how few have gratitude and love for Him, and how few ever tell Him that they love Him! Yet He has transformed us, as a dull crystal is transformed into flashing brilliancy when it catches the rays of the sun. Even so, by Him and by the life of grace which He sends us, are we transformed into children of God. "The charity of God is poured forth into our hearts by the Holy Ghost," wrote St. Paul to the Romans (5:5). Yes, for God is love, and above all the Holy Ghost is the manifestation of that love.

Call to mind the ecstatic cry of St. Paul at the beginning

of his Second Epistle to the Corinthians: "Blessed be the God and Father of Our Lord Jesus Christ, the Father of mercies and God of all comfort; who comforteth us in all our tribulation" (II Cor. 1:3). And this consolation He imparts to us through the workings of the Holy Ghost within us. Therefore in all our tribulations we shall be sustained by the Holy Spirit of God if we but go to Him with confidence and love. For the Holy Ghost, the Comforter, is ever with us, helping us to bear everything, and perfecting us by means of His gifts. Let us, therefore, go to Him in our troubles, have recourse to Him in all our tribulations, and so let these very tribulations be instruments for drawing us ever closer to God, for increasing our love of God, and for strengthening our faith in the ever-present help of God. Let us pray often that the Holy Ghost may perfect His work within us, and not only in us but also in all mankind, that so that change of heart which is so much needed today, which is, indeed, the only hope for the world in its present great distress and peril, may speedily by His promptings and inspirations become a blessed reality. In short, let us repeat yet again, but henceforth with all our heart and mind, that prayer which we so often, but unfortunately so thoughtlessly, say: "Send forth Thy Spirit and they shall be created; and Thou shalt renew the face of the earth."

XII

LOOKING AT LIFE

The mental attitude we adopt toward life is important, since it affects our general outlook, our spirits, and even our spiritual prospects; a false view of life can mislead and depress us, and result in a misunderstanding of God on our part. We have in this matter to realize, as well as to know, the fleeting and purely preparatory nature of life, that it is not our be-all and end-all, and that it is not even important except as regards how we behave in it. A right perspective of life enables us to grasp this view, and thereby to look on the events of life and the trials of humanity and to see them more as God sees them. And what is this right perspective? In a word, we have to understand that we are pilgrims merely passing through this world, wayfarers, not permanent dwellers here. Hence the true importance of life will be grasped if we view it as a preparation for something vastly more important; and the grievances, hardships, and disappointments that it brings will fall into their right place and will not assume exaggerated greatness.

It is most important that we should accustom ourselves to taking this larger, truer view of life, which is simply the stark reality. We are, as I say, pilgrims passing through, and so St. Paul reminds us that "we have not here a lasting city" (Heb. 13:14). That fact goes far to explain three-quarters of the mysteries and perplexities of life and of the workings of God's providence which sometimes seem strange to us. A thousand years is but as a moment to God, and our brief appearance in this world is flashing past. It is largely forgetfulness of this truth or failure to realize it fully that leads us to make wrong judgments on the events of life and its difficulties. Since we are journeying, we must expect the discomforts of travel. But they are only momentary. We shall be comfortable again when we reach home. Subconsciously, if not consciously, we are longing for home (everyone is), because our souls are made for God and cannot be happy without Him, as St. Augustine remarks. Hence, then, the dissatisfaction with life which all feel, even the wealthiest and the apparently most fortunate. And God intends us to feel this. He would not have us perfectly satisfied with this world, for then we would be in great danger of forgetting Him and the goal to which we are traveling. So it has been wisely remarked that "it would be dreadful if man were ever at peace here on earth," and that "the only dreadful thing in life is to be contented with life." Reflect on that provocative and star-tling saying. It is a divine discontent that shakes us up, keeps us restless, and prevents us from vegetating in for-getfulness of God.

We are, then, let me repeat, journeying, and until we get that view of life completely into our whole mentality we will always be misunderstanding life and God, and even criticizing Him, at least implicitly. Failure to have this right viewpoint accounts for much of the unbelief and blasphemy in the world. Man expects to be happy, he thinks he even has a right to be happy, and then if he does not get happiness he either considers God unjust or he denies God's existence altogether. But this attitude is based on an utter misconception, because in the first place the world is, and is intended to be, a place of trial, a place of conflict and victory (or defeat), not of peace and content; a place of testing, not of resting; a means, not an end. And in the second place it is all so fleeting that its pains and difficulties and disappointments, when viewed in the light of eternity and thus seen in their true proportions, matter little in comparison. This attitude is not callousness; it is simply seeing things in their true light, and is therefore true wisdom. To unbelievers, who do not believe in the next life, the agonies and "disasters" which many people encounter are stark tragedy; but for us, who have the outlook given by the Christian revelation, life's troubles and pains are robbed of three-quarters of their sting.

The same line of thought applies to the restless ambition and unsatisfied longings which disturb a great many. They feel their lives are thwarted and wasted; they are always planning and looking forward to what they will do some day. And thus from youth to old age the ideal circumstances seem to be just around the corner; but in reality those conditions never come, because fulfillment and perfect happiness were not intended for this life. They will come later, when our pilgrimage is over and we have "run the course." Our real home is on the other side of death. Here in this world we are perpetually in more or less of a muddle, as one generally is when traveling; and so it has been at all times, and ever will be. The fundamental mistake is for people to imagine that this life is what matters. We have, then, to try to realize why anything is important in this life. For each of us, events are important or unimportant only from heaven's viewpoint. The household drudge, the man denied opportunities of ever exercising his talents, the lifelong cripple: all these ask if such is to be their whole life, always doing petty tasks, always downtrodden, always suffering. And the answer is: No. While they continue to do or to suffer these things they are carrying out God's all-wise plans and thereby fulfilling their allotted part in the scheme of creation; but their real life is to see God face to face in heaven. There and then they will have full opportunities of "self-expression," and of living life in all its fullness.

Since we are thus pilgrims in a foreign land, it follows that we must not be surprised or disconcerted if we are looked on as being strange and eccentric, just as one is frequently regarded when one is traveling abroad. "My thoughts are not your thoughts, nor your ways My ways" (Isa. 55:8), said Almighty God to the worldly-wise, and similarly, in due proportion, the world's ways are not our ways, nor its ideals and thoughts our ideals and thoughts. Moreover we must see to it that, as far as we are concerned, this continues to be so. Of course we need courage and a strong spirituality to maintain this position and these differences, for we are strongly and persistently tempted to fall in with the world's ways. And courage is especially needed these days when world opinion is swayed by the newspapers, so that opinions are turned out by mass production, and the man in the street hardly dares to think for himself, or at the least is unwittingly influenced to a decisive extent by what he reads. We have a responsibility in this matter. The world needs the truth, and it is for us to maintain it, not only by our words, but still more by our way of life and by our outlook on life. The truth can be reached only by following Christ, and that not in the well-worn valleys, but over the bare mountain tops. Mockery and contempt was His lot upon earth, and often it is that of His followers also, as He foretold it would be. But if we follow Him faithfully whither He leads us, we know that our steps will bring us ultimately in safety to our eternal home. For He is "the way, the truth, and the life."

Yet, although the worldly look upon us as being "different," they experience, as I have said, a restlessness, a dissatisfaction with the world, and this dissatisfaction is of divine origin and is part of God's plan. Mankind alone possesses it; the rest of creation is placid and fulfills its purpose. But something has happened to man, or rather something has been added to him, and that something is grace, which has changed our souls from having merely natural life (though immortal) to having supernatural life. The greater part of the New Testament is devoted to showing the establishment of this grace in us and describing its effects. In brief, by it we have become kinsmen of God, supernaturalized, and heirs of heaven; therefore we are unsatisfied without God. Grace enables us to acquire a true knowledge of God; and to know God is to love Him and to long for Him. Therefore the greater our grace (and hence the holier our lives), the more we long for heaven. Hence also the indifference shown to God by the thoroughly worldly, for they have lost grace by their worldly lives. Cherish, then, this divine discontent by increasing your grace (through faithful correspondence with that which you have), and by meditating often on your future home in the city of eternal life. By grace we share in the divine nature; and we are sensitive to God and to His impulses within us, so that our souls vibrate in harmony with His will.

Realizing, then, the cause and purpose of this dissatisfaction that we have with life, we should realize also that mere doing of things, mere action, of which the world makes such a fetish, is of little consequence. On a journey one generally does not do much. That is one reason why there are so many apparently colorless lives. We are not necessarily meant to do things, except what God happens to send us to do.

They also serve who only stand and wait

for they are doing God's will, and thus fulfilling the object of life. Our real achievements will be in the next life, and will make the activities of this life seem emptiness and idleness. That is one reason why the contemplative saints are content to let the world go by, using this life only to make preparation for the next world. And the active saints, too, understand the futility and nothingness of mere activity apart from God. This is true of all religious, but it is most obvious in the purely contemplative orders, for their members have finished with life, and their whole existence is but a preparation for death.

Looking at life in this way, seeing it as merely a short journey, helps us to be indifferent to it with that holy indifference which leaves everything to God, and subordinates our will entirely to the divine will, so that we desire nothing else. This state was well described by St. Francis de Sales, and he said of it: "Our will cannot die any more than our mind can, but it sometimes goes beyond the limits of ordinary life, in order to live utterly and entirely in the will of God. It then neither wills nor desires anything, but casts itself absolutely on the good pleasure of God, and is so thoroughly imbued and penetrated with His will that it seems to have no separate existence, but to be hidden with Christ in God." And he himself attained to this self-abandonment by practice. He tells us, indeed, that he learnt the lesson in his youth, and that if he had to live his life over again he would let himself be ruled by Providence in even the smallest things with childlike simplicity and deep contempt for all human wisdom. When in physical danger, as when one day crossing stormy Lake Geneva in a frail boat, he felt unspeakable delight in realizing that his life was so utterly in God's hands. All of us must have felt a somewhat similar delight when we first came to the religious life and realized that henceforth all the details of our life would be directly regulated and settled by God through our superiors. So have we sure guidance on our journey through life, or rather our journey toward life, and thus are we saved from the quicksands or swamps on either side of the road.

And if this view of life helps us to abandon ourselves to God in that way, and to maintain that attitude, we can further fortify ourselves in it by often reflecting on His wisdom, power, and love, which give us every reason for absolute confidence in Him. We can meditate also on His promises to us, such as those contained in the beautiful parable of the lilies of the field and the birds of the air. And we can confirm ourselves in this by actually giving ourselves to Him once more, by renewing our vows, leaving Him to do with us as He chooses, remembering St. Paul's words: "Know you not . . . you are not your own? For you are bought with a great price" (I Cor. 6:20), namely, the blood of Christ. We are, indeed, by reason of our vows, and also by our redemption, not our own property, and so we must make the complete holocaust of ourselves. Many who desire to belong to God wish to be their own property also; but God will have no half-measures.

And if this state of self-abandonment is to become real to us, we must often renew the act by which we have given all to God, remembering the day of our profession and the fervor and earnestness and generosity we then felt. If we cannot actually feel now the same fervor, as is very proba-

ble, we can tell God that we none the less ratify and confirm now what we did then, and that, if we had never
given ourselves to Him entirely by our vows, we would
do so now. That is a most meritorious and fruitful practice, and it also moves us to accept all that happens as
being a favor from Him. And all this we must do, this life
of faith we must lead, without heeding the outcries of nature. "As to feelings," writes the great doctor of Geneva,
"I do not waste any time over them." In these dispositions,
then, we will bravely and profitably travel our journey
through life, seeing all things in their true perspective, and
taking as our guide this excellent advice of a certain holy
nun: "Do not go back upon the past, do not speculate on
the future, and for the present only keep close to God."
Look at life with the eyes of eternity, and you will see all
things rightly.

XIII

TRANQUILLITY

In the previous chapter we said that most of our unhappiness in this world is owing to our mental attitude toward life. We may now add that the remainder, although it has a solid basis of reality, can yet be turned to a bitter-sweet joy which is even more valuable than unalloyed joy. For happiness or unhappiness is promoted, not by what happens, but by the view we take, since happiness and unhappiness are matters that are largely subjective. All of which is another way of saying that, if we live by spiritual principles, we can find joy in anything and everything, knowing that it all comes, directly or indirectly, from God, and that therefore its very unpleasantness is profitable to us, holy, and pleasing to God; and consequently it becomes delightful to ourselves. But the extent to which we can make this attitude ours depends on the depth and the reality of our spiritual life, and the degree to which we have assimilated the truths of religion.

This is not a stage to be reached at once, for it requires strenuous endeavor, but when it is attained we have tranquillity, perfect mental peace, no matter what happens; and that is a priceless gift. Then external events can have no influence on the superior part of the soul, even though outwardly we may appear disturbed; just as in stormy weather there is a rough sea on the surface of the ocean, yet there is always calm in the depths. And this is our attitude because, as I have suggested, happiness is a condition of mind, and not a disposition of circumstances. Circumstances can be a means of happiness (of a sort); but to depend on them for happiness would be to sacrifice the reality of happiness for the sake of the supposed means to happiness, as millions do. Moreover, true happiness can in the nature of things rest only on God, who is unchanging, dependable, and not liable to the vicissitudes of human affairs. And thus in Him we find perfect peace, and from the bitter fountains of His passion we learn to delight in trials and adversities, having unshaken serenity, for we know that God allows only what is for our ultimate good and His own glory, that these difficulties strengthen our souls and have not only disciplinary but also impetratory value, and that we are privileged by them to participate in His sufferings and so to purify our souls and also those of others.

Many, of course, never reach this stage; with some, attainment to it is the work of a lifetime; but others rapidly reach it, and such have generally many trials sent them to test and strengthen their new-found fortitude and tranquillity. Again God gives to some souls sensible tranquillity, a feeling of peace, despite all life's buffetings; while others have this tranquillity in reality, yet they are much troubled in the lower part of their souls and externally. Of these two forms the latter is preferable, because it is hardier and is devoid of the consolations of the former. In this respect it is somewhat akin to that absence of consolation in prayer, complete aridity, loneliness to the point of breaking, and apparent desertion by God, which has been the experience of many of the saints; and it leads to heroic virtue if it is borne patiently and lovingly. St. Teresa of Lisieux experienced the extreme of desolation, and practically never felt any joy or love in the religious life, yet she said: "I do not wish love that I can feel; if Jesus can feel it, then that is enough." This is true heroism, and it is typical of her so-called "Little Way," which is really her great way, for there is nothing little about it except the material from which it was constructed. It calls for the practice of heroic self-conquest in even the smallest things of daily life, and perseverance in that course.

We should note, too, that preservation of cheerfulness and tranquillity were a prominent feature of her "way." Therefore it will not be out of place if we dwell on that way for a moment in passing. It was ambitious and thoroughgoing, and involved persistent ruthlessness toward self. In it the feelings and inclinations must never be shown, and hence all her companions thought her happy and at peace, while in reality her soul was torn with anguished doubt and scruples. Yet her "night of the spirit" was never allowed to show itself in her bearing, though she herself said: "It is no longer a curtain, it is a wall between me and the starry firmament. I feel no joy when I sing of the happiness of heaven and the eternal possession of God, for I am singing only of that which I want to believe." Probably many of us have experienced the same trial, and therefore we find comfort in the knowledge that this great saint felt the same. An occasional ray of sunshine had to satisfy her for long months on end. But her "Little Way" consisted in triumphing over this interior dejection and all other manifestations of self-will. Martyrdom itself is sometimes a less prolonged trial than this; martyrdom calls for only one triumph over the flesh, and is followed by immediate reward, whereas her way of life required continual triumph at terrible cost. Its essence was to put great deeds at the service of small things, which involves what she calls a "denudation" in which a soul feels itself at the breaking-point, and a renouncing of all concessions to self and of all happiness, even spiritual happiness, if God so demands, as He did in her case. In view of all this we are not surprised when we are told that St. John of the Cross was her favorite author. She was nourished on his writings. Yet amid all these trials of the spirit and the exercise of heroic endurance she had tranquillity and deep abiding peace beneath all the storms.

But most of us do not experience so sore a trial as this, and we should be able to preserve our peace of mind, not only in the depths of the soul but also on the surface. Mere outward circumstances, however trying, should never be able to ruffle even the surface calm of a truly spiritual soul: only spiritual torment can do that. In the ordinary affairs of life, however complex or painful they may be, the religious can and should maintain tranquillity of thought and demeanor, realizing the transient nature of all such troubles, and having the peace of God within her and being completely dominated by it. The peace of a good conscience, the joy of serving God faithfully come what may, and the knowledge that we are fulfilling His holy will: these things dwarf everything else in our eyes. This unshakable peace is a precious possession which we must allow nothing to take from us. It is our sheet-anchor in life, our trusty armor against the wiles of the devil at the hour of our death, and our passport into the joys of eternity. It is the peace that the world cannot give, of which Our Lord says: "My peace I give unto you."

But this peace is acquired generally only at the cost of persistent effort and earnest prayer, and only after we have attained to some measure of detachment. For obviously it cannot be ours while we are mentally still at the mercy of the ups and downs of daily life, but only when we are indifferent to these so that they can no longer depress or elate us. Hence the need for self-discipline. St. Thomas Aquinas tells us: "Man is placed between earthly objects and spiritual good in which eternal beatitude consists; the closer he adheres to the one the further he is removed from the other." When one end of the scale rises, the other goes down. Since original sin has made this matter very difficult for us, we have what Abbot Chautard calls "the arduous task of constantly tearing away from earthly thoughts and aspirations, by dint of watchfulness, self-denial, and mortification, that heart of ours which is borne down by the immense weight of our corrupt nature, and of making an unreserved holocaust of all attachment to creatures, of all merely natural desires, and of our self-will and judgment."

Unfortunately all this is more easily said than done, for those are the very things most difficult for us to shed. Yet this painful amputation has to be made if we are really to belong to God and to reap in full measure the graces which He is waiting to bestow on us, if, indeed, we are to be faithful followers of Him at all. Let us not think we can escape this sacrifice and yet be happy in God's service. It cannot be done. We must be either seeking self or seeking God; we cannot do both. In this matter, then, we need clear intellectual sight, that we may see things as they really are; our prospects may be considerably handicapped if we should suffer from scruples, for these blind the judgment of the sufferer and destroy his peace. Then one can but hang on grimly, forcing oneself to make acts of faith and hope, and of complete abandonment into the hands of God. But scruples may be known by the fact that they tend to produce despair, thus showing that they are not from God. Warnings from God never have that effect, nor do they produce violent commotion. "Everything that destroys the peace and tranquillity of the interior proceeds from the devil. God has joined together happiness and holiness in such wise that His graces not only sanctify the soul, but also console it, and fill it with peace and sweetness. The suggestions of the devil have the very contrary effect. The serpent is known by his tail, i.e., by the effects he produces and the conclusion to which he leads." [1]

We must, then, seek peace of mind and resolutely put away mental disturbances. One of the surest ways of doing this is by means of humility, because peace is to be found in giving way, in not asserting ourselves or our opinions. This humility is not weakness; on the contrary, it is strength, for often great strength of mind and iron self-control are required to carry it out. It is, in fact, with some strong natures, little short of heroic thus to overcome their natural inclinations, and it is the way of the saints, part of the Via Dolorosa which we have to learn to tread, and which can nowhere be learnt better than in the religious life wherein so many opportunities of practicing it are daily given. "To lead a quiet, humble, peaceable interior life of personal love with Our Lord, not caring what other people do, think, or say, is the only way of happiness," [2] and, we may add, of holiness also.

Earnest spirits can attain to this only after a hard course of discipline that trains them to develop their interior life, to govern themselves ruthlessly, and not to allow themselves to be ruled by external circumstances, but on the contrary to subject all their faculties to their will, and their will entirely to the holy will of God. This is a hard battle, but a necessary one, and beyond it lies awaiting us the prize of peace, perfect tranquillity of mind and heart, the peace that passeth all understanding and enables us to run in the way of God.

[1] Father Lallemant.
[2] Father Bertrand Wilberforce, O.P.

XIV

NOVITIATE PRINCIPLES

Let us today go back in spirit to the novitiate, and recall some of those elementary principles which were dinned into us when we were novices. I trust you will not turn up your nose at such an idea, since to do so would be a sure sign of pride and of self-satisfaction. If indeed you are so disposed, then that very fact would make it all the more necessary to go back to novitiate principles. In fact, almost all religious would be improved and helped by having a second novitiate somewhere about the time of their silver jubilee. One thing more by way of introduction: let no one think that these principles are unimportant. On the contrary, they are of the utmost importance: that is why they are taught to us at the beginning of our religious life. They are the foundations without which we cannot build the spiritual edifice. The foundations are the most indispensable part of any building, they have to endure throughout the life of the building. These principles may not be forgotten or neglected once we have left the novitiate behind. For they are vital throughout our life, and just as necessary now as when we first learnt them. In view of all this, then, no apology is needed for reverting to them now.

In the novitiate it often happens that we have to be corrected (that, after all, is the object of the novitiate), and it sometimes happens that in later life we also need correction. But, while we take it for granted that a novice is docile and meekly accepts correction, and also that she has the sense to know that correction is a necessary part of her training, and therefore welcomes it as being for her own good, the case is not always so simple with older religious. Unfortunately growth in sanctity and in the extirpation of self does not invariably correspond with growth in age, and thus it happens that occasionally an older religious, who ought to know better, resents correction and, worse still, lets it be seen that she resents it. What folly that is, and what harm it does! Harm above all to herself, but also great harm to others by the bad example and disedification she thereby gives. As for the folly of it: is it not folly to refuse the medicine that God offers for our healing? Healing, by pointing out our faults, and also healing by thus humiliating us and so helping us to crush ourselves and to gain merit and grace. What folly not to thank God for it, and to seize the golden opportunity for increasing our graces by accepting the correction humbly and joyfully, even if it should not be deserved! In fact, if we are unjustly rebuked, we are yet more fortunate, for our self-restraint and humility in accepting such a rebuke is far more meritorious and valuable than if the correction had been deserved. That being so, we can see how foolish and wrong it is to resent a correction which has been deserved.

But now, it is after all quite understandable, in view of

what human nature is, for an older religious so to act (unwise and imperfect though such conduct be). But, in a sense it is much worse for a novice to do this, since the whole purpose of a young person in entering the novitiate is that she may be trained to walk in the way of God, and training is necessarily a forcible and painful process: nothing less than the eradication of self and of the petty indulging of self for which human nature clamors. Pride, self-will, and the like, have to be ruthlessly rooted out; that is the object of the novitiate; or at least the process of rooting out those things has to be begun in the novitiate. If, therefore, she did not wish to be corrected, the novice should never have come to the religious life. We come not to do our own will but that of God as shown to us by our superiors. Let us, then, never resent any rebuke, even though it come from an equal or from one who is below us in rank; to do so is to show that we are still full of pride, still unmortified, still untrained. And not only should we not resent it, but we should not be upset by it. Let us take it to heart, but never be disturbed by it. We must acknowledge our fault promptly, receive the rebuke with gratitude (for it is a favor from God), and offer to God the interior humiliation and distress it causes. Then we ought to forget about it, and not mope over it or dwell on it; to do so is to play the devil's game. Let us rise up and begin again, with all our trust in God and none in ourselves. In that way we shall turn the rebuke into precious gold; this was what God intended us to do with it, and why He sent it.

And now there naturally follows the next point, which is that we should never make excuses, no matter how good or humanly justified they may be. How sad it is to see a religious making excuses and thereby flinging away the opportunity of meriting, and the graces and rewards which God is offering her! How God loathes excuses! After all, why do we seek to excuse ourselves? Practically always from pride and self-love, our two greatest enemies. Why, then, pander to those enemies, and thereby strengthen them? For the offering of an excuse does not make us any better in God's eyes. He knows already what justification we had, and we are as we are. Excuses will not improve us; on the contrary, they harm us, as we have just seen. There can be but one other reason, as a rule, for making them: a desire to stand better in the eyes of the one who corrects or rebukes us. But that again is a wrong policy and a harmful snare. For what is it but pride again that makes us seek to be well thought of by superiors? The saints sought to be despised, imitating Him who was "despised and rejected of men"; yet we seek to be esteemed, and therefore we feebly make excuses. What folly and what weakness this is! By biting back the excuse that rises to our lips, we shall not only gain merit and give edification, but will also immensely strengthen our own character, and deal a hard blow at our mortal enemy, namely, ourselves and our self-love.

And this mention of the evils flowing from pride leads one inevitably to think of its opposite, humility. What a glorious exercise of humility we have in this matter of refraining from making excuses, and how many other opportunities we have every day of exercising this virtue in other ways! Few things endear us so much to God as humility. Indeed, it is one of the chief things He looks for in us, since without it we cannot please Him. Our Lady tells us that He exalts the humble and casts down the proud, and it was her own humility which brought the archangel Gabriel to her with his heaven-shaking announcement. Yes, this virtue storms the heart of God and draws rich graces from Him. If we are humble, much else may be forgiven us; but if we are not humble, we are not a religious at all. "Be ye humbled under the mighty hand of God," says the Apostle; and then we shall have gone far toward rooting out self-will, for "pride doth its own will, humility doth the will of God." Moreover, if we are humble, the other virtues will almost automatically follow.

It has just been said that humility will help us to root out self-will. Self-will: what an abominable and poisonous thing it is! It is above all to exterminate self-will that we come to the religious life, for we come to do the will of God. And this is of paramount importance since it is the foundation stone of the religious life; yet its achievement is most painful to human nature. That is the chief reason why the novitiate is, or should be, a painful place, for it is the dentist's chair in which self-will has to be forcibly extracted. If our self-will has not been well mortified and greatly weakened during our novitiate, then that novitiate has been wasted and has failed in its primary purpose.

Self-will is the root of sin; its destruction is the prerequisite of virtue. That is why the religious loves the religious life, because in it she knows that all day she is, by virtue of holy obedience, doing God's will and not her own. Therein we see at once the charm and the supreme value of the life. And that, too, is why a good religious shrinks from expressing a preference and likes to leave the choice to superiors. And also that is why she never shows the slightest shadow of reluctance to obey an order, because to do so would be to pander once again to self-will and so to lose the fruits of so much labor and mortification in the past. One could not imagine a fervent religious showing reluctance to obey or expressing distaste for a task, for that would be such crass folly, as well as displeasing to God. If we wish to do only what we like, that is, to do only our own will, why did we come to the religious life at all? No, like our divine Master we say: "I came down from heaven, not to do my own will, but the will of Him that sent me" (John 6:38); or, in our case, "the will of Him that called me."

In so doing we are being sensible, for God can make full use of us only when He has fashioned us afresh, when He has molded our wills so that they are in accord with His. Abbot Marmion [1] remarks, in this connection, that if a statue is to be made out of a block of marble, the block must first be whittled down and chipped, and that when we enter the religious life we are like the block of marble. If anything is to be made of us, we have to be subjected

[1] *Christ the Ideal of the Monk.*

to the painful process of being chipped by the chisel of
God wielded by our superiors. And Father Caussade uses
precisely the same simile. Obviously that all means a complete disregard of self-will, an annihilation of it; and we
bring that about by exact and meticulous obedience to
the instructions of those set over us.

It is surprising how, as time goes on, one tends to begin
growing slack about obedience. Not that a religious is ever
grossly or flagrantly disobedient. God forbid! But there is
likely to be a tendency after some years to be less careful
in the matter; to put off fulfilling a command; to do it in
our own way; perhaps even to question, if not in words at
least in thought, the wisdom of a command. But all that
will not do. Let us recall why we obey: we obey because
we know it is the voice of God speaking through His
deputy; because also we know that obedience is the way
of salvation, since by it we are assured of doing God's will;
and because also we have vowed obedience. That being
so, it follows that our obedience must be blind, instant,
and ungrudging.[2] Let us take those qualities in turn. We
do not obey merely because we approve of, or like, the
order or task given to us, but because God has spoken.
And for the same reason we do not delay setting about it,
and therefore, in military parlance, we "jump to it"; and
we do not obey unwillingly, also for the same reason,
and because we know that grudging it would spoil
the whole thing, and smirch the offering we are mak-

[2] St. Benedict, dealing in his Rule with the interior qualities which obedience must have, says that it must be supernatural, confidant, and loving,
that is, it must be based on faith, hope, and charity.

ing to God, who "loveth a cheerful giver" (II Cor. 9:7).

And now to conclude, the gist of what has been said above is, "Spiritualize, spiritualize, spiritualize." And this refers not only to our general intention in all our work (it is most important always to do all our work, irrespective of what it may be, from a spiritual motive, that is, for love of God), but also to all our thoughts and to our outlook on life. All these must have a spiritual tinge. Therefore let us do nothing from merely natural motives, or simply by way of routine, or even merely because it needs doing. To act thus is to lose much of the merit of the deed and to prevent it from being an offering to God. No matter how menial, unimportant, or "indifferent" an action may seem, if it is done with a spiritual motive it is an act of worship and of love, and is therefore pleasing to God and profitable to our soul. But if our daily tasks are done merely from a spirit of routine (and there is always a danger of that), great harm is done to the soul, and the labor is not acceptable to God. And this applies perhaps particularly to lay sisters, for the temptation to that danger is especially great with them owing to the nature of their tasks; but it also applies to choir religious. We should, then, spiritualize everything, and see everything that befalls us in a spiritual light, taking all that happens to us, whether directly from God or by way of our superiors, our equals, or those beneath us in rank, in a spiritual manner. By that means we will transform our mind, we will transform our soul, and we will also help to transform the souls of others. What greater inducement than that could we desire?

XV

THE DIVINE OFFICE

The human heart, when it is not utterly estranged from God, especially the heart of the religious, feels an imperative call to worship, praise, and thank God, and it receives from doing so an interior joy that nothing else can give. This demand of our nature the Church, of course, fully realizes, and partly in order to satisfy it and partly because this worship is a strict obligation placed on us by God, she has provided the perfect means of fulfilling it by the sacred liturgy, that is, by the Mass and the Divine Office. It is to the latter that I would draw your attention now: the official liturgical prayer of the Church. What follows applies to you whether in your Order you say the complete Office, or whether you recite a much shorter form of Office, such as the Little Office of the Blessed Virgin.

Of course the great principle to grasp is that the Office is the official public prayer of the Church, it is the Church herself praying. Partly because of that, and partly because of the communion of saints, by which we are all one with Christ and with the saints in heaven, it follows that when we say our Office, even in private, we are not praying alone. We are united with the innumerable host of adorers on earth and in heaven, so that not only does our prayer help to swell the mighty chorus of praise ascending to the Throne, but also the prayers of all the faithful throughout the world are added to, or rather are one with, our own prayer and therefore greatly increase its power. This is one reason why the Office is so potent a prayer (much more so than any private prayer that we make) and why it is so pleasing to God and such a vastly important duty, or rather privilege, on our part.

We have just said that the Divine Office is the Church herself praying; but it is also more than that, because it is Christ Himself praying, for not only is God the author of the Office since it comes almost entirely from the inspired Scriptures, but also Christ as the Head of the Church offers up to His Father the worship presented by His members. This is the second reason for the importance and potency of the Divine Office. Such, then, is the prayer which God Himself has given us, which He has written, in which it is He Himself praying, and which brings us into close communication with Him. Moreover, the value of any action depends on the object for which it is done and to which it is directed; but in this particular case that to which our action is directed is God; hence it is the noblest and highest of occupations. When one is saying one's Office, even privately, one is doing the greatest, most valuable, and most exalted thing that any human person can do, except only celebrating Mass. When, therefore, you see someone saying his Office, realize that he is doing something sublime, that he is bringing down on mankind inestimable boons, the graces of God, and that, though apparently alone, he is in reality surrounded by the countless adoring hosts of heaven. Greater far than to govern empires or to civilize whole nations is the action of one who devoutly says his Office.

When we reflect that the primary object of man's creation is that he should worship and praise God, and when we recall the necessity and also the immense motives of love and gratitude which we have for doing so, we might reasonably expect that all mankind would spend a large part of every day offering this worship. But worldliness and coldness, ignorance and sin, have combined to prevent this; consequently millions never think of God, and even devout Christians can in fact give but little time to Him, immersed as they are in their affairs. Therefore it is that at a very early age of its history the Church set apart certain people to whom she entrusted this duty of constant prayer not only for themselves but also on behalf of those who could not or would not themselves give so much time to it. Thus it has been that she has ever since charged the clergy and all professed religious with the duty and privilege of daily reciting the Divine Office, either in choir or privately, and so maintaining forever the unbroken sequence of praise ascending from earth to heaven. In this way also these chosen ones emulate the Psalmist, who proclaimed: "Seven times a day I have given praise to Thee" (Ps. 118:164). For just so does the religious praise God seven times daily: Matins and Lauds during the night, Prime at break of day, Terce, Sext, and None at their three respective hours, sixthly Vespers at eventide, and seventhly Compline, which is the Church's night prayers. Thus does the Church militant unite herself daily with the Church triumphant in paying to the infinite Majesty of the Most High her rightful and official homage of praise and adoration, of gratitude and love.

This being so, it is no wonder that in some orders the recitation or chanting of the Office is the primary object of the institute, as, for instance, in the Benedictine Order, wherein it has always been one main occupation of the life. In his Holy Rule, St. Benedict, after laying down lengthy and minute regulations about how the Office (which he always refers to as "the Work of God") is to be recited or sung, says flatly: "Let nothing be placed before the Work of God." Whatever else may have to be cut short, the Office must be kept up in full; to see to that is the main purpose of a monk's life, any other work he may undertake being secondary to it. Thus his task is "to do on earth what the angels do in heaven," that is, to maintain the psalmody. And, in truth, if one has worthily and conscientiously sung God's praises all one's life, has not one's time been admirably spent? Cultivate, then, and foster all your life a great devotion to and appreciation of your holy Office. And if in some orders the Office that is said is much shorter than the full Office of the Church, that is all the more reason for saying it carefully and devoutly. The Divine Office is a solid, safe, and powerful devotion, with no frills or fancy-work about it, no cloying sentiment as in some modern devotions. It is dignified and all-sufficing, the official devotion of the Church.

But what is meant when we say that the Office should be recited carefully and devoutly? To answer this we must come down to details, for there are several different methods possible, all of which are excellent according to our various temperaments and abilities. But let me preface what may be said on that subject by quoting the preliminary prayer in the Breviary, which has to be recited daily before beginning the Office. Translated it runs: "Open, O Lord, my mouth to bless Thy holy name; cleanse also my heart from all vain, perverse, and alien thoughts; enlighten my intellect, inflame my affections, that I may worthily, attentively, and devoutly recite this Office, and that I may deserve to be heard before the face of Thy divine Majesty, through Christ Our Lord. Amen." Therein you find the dispositions we should have at our Office: worthily, attentively, devoutly, is the way the Church would have us say it. But how precisely should we do this? Let us see what are the possibilities.

And first of all let us be clear that, should it happen you do not understand Latin, this does not detract from the value of your offering of the Office, though of course you yourself appreciate it much more and so draw more fervor from it if you do understand it. But even if you do not, you are using the inspired words and making them your own, and moreover you intend that the dispositions expressed by them be yours also. You are thus fully able to unite yourself to God by the Office, even though the sense of the words be not understood. The divine words of the Holy Ghost have just as much power as if you understood their meaning. It is your intention that matters. And, speaking of intention, let me remind you to have always a specific intention for which you offer each portion of the Office. Do not waste this opportunity of offering powerful prayer for the special intentions which you have at heart.

Now we come to the equally important matter of the attention we should have when reciting our Office. Of course we must give it some attention of the mind, otherwise it is not prayer and becomes merely a gabble which is an insult to God. Hence the gross impropriety of deliberate distractions during the Office. But several different kinds of attention are possible, and what follows is the teaching of Father Augustine Baker, the seventeenth-century Benedictine, in his famous book *Sancta Sophia*. Therein he mentions three degrees of attention, or three ways of attending, of which the lowest and easiest is that of actual reflection on the words and their meaning as we recite them. This, though good, has the defect that, since the words and sentiments are continually succeeding one another, we cannot fix the mind for any length of time on any one thought, or unite ourselves powerfully or effectively with God. Thus this method is too disturbing and unstable. Father Baker declares that "the more imperfect we are, the less difficulty we find in giving this attention; for souls which have good and established affections to God can hardly (i.e., only with difficulty) quit a good affection by which they are united to God to exchange it for a new one succeeding in the Office," and that it would be bad for them if they did.

His second degree is that of those who, accustomed to internal prayer, continue in recollection during the Office and ignore the meaning of the words. This method is far more beneficial than the former, and it would be wrong for anyone to desert it for the former, since the object of vocal prayer is to furnish the soul with affections which will unite it to God, and therefore one who is already so united by recollection should not seek the inferior means offered by attention to the words.

But the third and highest degree of attention is that by which the vocal prayers become mental prayer, i.e., that in which souls who are thus united to God can at the same time attend to the sense of the words without prejudice to this union and, in fact, find their affection and union increased by the meaning of the psalms. But generally this stage is not reached until we have arrived at perfect contemplation, and it is experienced by but few. Those, then, are the three methods of reciting the Office described by Father Baker.

But, whatever method we adopt, our aim should be to be attentive and devout, remembering the vision of St. Bernard in which he saw above the choir a group of angels who were recording the words as they were recited by each religious, some of which were taken down in letters of gold, some in silver, and some only in water, according to the degree in which the monks were attending to what

they were saying or were in union with God. Nor is this
unreasonable, for prayers uttered thoughtlessly and in-
attentively are not worthy to be recorded and are indeed
an affront to God.

Now let me finally recall to you once more the high
esteem and love you should always have for your Office.
"Psalterium meum, gaudium meum." [1] When you stand
in choir before the holy of holies to give God this prayer
and praise in union with the heavenly choirs which unite
their voices with yours, you are expiating to God for the
indifference and neglect that is shown to Him by the great
mass of mankind. You are, as it were, chosen victims, but
highly privileged ones, and you are performing an invaluable work for the human race, because it is the Divine
Office which, with the Mass, turns away the wrath of God
from sinful man. You are echoing the song of praise that
rose first from the Sacred Heart of Jesus when He was
upon earth, and you are doing so in the words that God
Himself has chosen. Look beyond, then, the chapel in
which you pray; look beyond your own scanty numbers;
look up, look up, and see the vast unnumbered host on
earth and in heaven, lovers of God and faithful adorers,
who with the seraphim and cherubim fall down before
the Throne with the unceasing cry of "Holy, Holy, Holy,
Lord God Almighty," of which vast choir you form an
integral part. Think, too, of the many cathedrals, monasteries, and convents which for nearly two thousand years
have maintained unceasingly the Divine Office under that

[1] St. Augustine.

leadership and headship of Christ which gives the liturgical choir its official position. Reflect that always, night and day, somewhere in the world that blessed and holy chant of praise and adoration is rising up to the most high God.

What greater privilege could you wish on earth than to be thus permitted to take your part in this immense choir of heaven and earth? What happier duty could you fulfill? In what nobler occupation could you spend your time? And on your lips are the words that have been sanctified by centuries of use on the part of innumerable saints, words that have resounded in the catacombs of ancient Rome, that have risen up in the starlit night of the desert and the sun-baked noonday of the eastern hermitages as the anchorites and monks of old praised their Creator and hymned their King; words that have inflamed and consoled martyrs, confessors, priests, pontiffs, and virgins down the ages, and that the Holy Ghost Himself put into their mouths. By the Divine Office the world becomes one vast temple ever resounding the praises of the Most High, and to you Holy Church entrusts the task and the joy of maintaining that eternal song of love and worship. To do so perfectly, we cannot aspire; to do so negligently or with tepidity, we dare not. With the Psalmist we say to our beloved God: "How sweet are Thy words to my palate!" (Ps. 118:103.) We whose care and joy on earth it has been thus to sound daily the praises of God will find in heaven that the praising of our Creator will be our superabundant reward. *Sit laus Deo semper!* May God be forever praised!

XVI

PAST, PRESENT, AND FUTURE

Father Stanton wrote: "The past is our sanctuary, the present is our opportunity, the future is our hope."

From time to time we all feel an impulse to cast our minds both backwards and forwards: backwards in thanksgiving and in contrition, and forwards in hope and in confidence. Our memory tells us how God has watched over us in the past, while it also tells us how badly we have served Him; and our faith assures us that He will equally guard and guide us in the future and that we shall have the grace to serve Him better. The events, the trials, the difficulties, the joys, and the triumphs that are to come are hidden from us in the mysterious providence of God. But whatever they may be, and however they may affect us, we gladly and gratefully accept them all in advance as coming from His merciful hand, and revealing to us His all-holy will. May His name be ever praised.

Past, present, and future are all woven together into one design in the mind of God, and the fullness of that design is hidden from our eyes. Yet on looking back we can now at least see something of how that divine plan was working in and through us, even though at the time it was inexplicable to us. And thus the events of our past life have a precious quality, and it is justly that they have been described, as quoted at the beginning of this chapter, as forming the sanctuary of the soul. For they are the setting in which the operations of God were fulfilled in us, and they hold much that is private and sacred to each individual soul. The past has witnessed so many secret workings of God in each soul, and it enshrines so many divine graces lavished on each soul, that no matter how many failings, falls, even grave sins, it may contain, it is in a real sense sacred to us and a sanctuary for us.

But when we look back and consider our own individual past, whether the recent past or that of our whole life up to the present, it is easy to take a mistaken view of it. For not only is there the well-known fact that nobody can be a fair judge in his own case, but also there are two mistakes into one or other of which we are liable to fall. Of these two opposite extremes, one is to gloss over our falls, vaguely hoping for the best at the hands of God; the opposing mistake is to dwell too much on past sins, to brood over them, and thus to risk being led in the end down the way that leads to despair and destruction. Both those mistakes can have serious effects on a soul. Even if they do not produce actually disastrous results, they can at the least gravely hamper the soul's progress toward God.

With regard to the first of these errors, taking too light a view of our sins, we should turn our past to our spiritual profit by taking a warning from it with regard to our frailty and our liability to fall, by learning a true humility from it, so that we put our confidence not in ourselves but in God's help, and by exercising watchfulness and determination for the future. In this way our past failures can be stepping-stones for us to higher things and thereby be, as it were, causes in a certain sense of our ultimate salvation, and a source of strength and even comfort to us. We should not, therefore, dismiss them entirely from our minds, for they contain a lesson and a warning. "Be not without fear of forgiven sin," Scripture exhorts us. Moreover, we have to remember that these sins, although forgiven, may still call for reparation. We should, then, strive to forestall our purgatory, paying the price in this life by penance and by gaining indulgences.

For all these reasons we cannot afford to dismiss past sins altogether; but we must also avoid the opposite mistake of dwelling too much on them, because this can do much harm. For most religious it is best not to dwell on the thought of past sins after they have been confessed and after we have learnt from them the lesson of humility and of dependence on God. After all, they are no longer on our souls but have been washed away by the precious blood applied to us in the sacrament of penance; and God would have us happy and not miserable. This does not, of course, mean that we should not be contrite. Contrition, true compunction of heart, is essential, but that is in no way incompatible with happiness; indeed it produces happiness and is an element in any true happiness. Therefore never let yourself be depressed by past failures.[1] Cast

---

[1] "It is easier for God to forgive a past sin, than it is for a man or a woman to forget it." Father Strappini, S.J.

them into the boundless mercy of God, and bravely face
the future with the assurance of His forgiveness and His
help henceforth. God can and does bring good out of evil,
and by our very sins He can teach us to be humble, cau-
tious in avoiding the occasions of sins, prompt in applying
the remedies, patient in tribulation, full of confident hope
for the future, and above all charitable toward the failings
and sins of others through sad knowledge of our own
weakness in the past. Consequently, with regard to the
past, the point is not so much what we have done amiss,
as rather whether we have profited by it and learnt the
lesson.

And now, if the past is our sanctuary, the present is our
opportunity. In that fact we always have grounds for encouragement and hope. We can make better use of the
present than we have made of the past, and God is giving
us this extra chance. Now is the time, as St. Paul says, to
arise from sleep and to put on the armor of light. But the
present is fleeting, and each passing minute is weighted
with consequences for eternity, either good or bad. Let us
be sure, then, to use the present to the utmost of our power
for it will never return, and each moment, each opportunity, wasted has gone forever. Remember the old saying: "I will pass this way but once. If therefore there is
anything that I can do, let me do it now, for I shall not
pass this way again." At almost every moment of the day
God gives us a chance to do something meritorious, to
store up more treasure for ourselves in heaven. But often
we let the chance slip: the chance, for instance, to help a

brother or sister, to say a kind word, to perform an act of self-denial, to make a brief ejaculation of love or of faith. Time is flying fast, and the present is our opportunity; the motto, "do it now," is worth many vague resolutions for the future.

If, then, the past is our sanctuary and the present our opportunity, surely it is equally true that the future is our hope. For the future lies still unspoiled, a clean sheet of paper with as yet no blots on it. We can use it as we like. It is for us either to spot it or to keep it clean. Let us think of that well. The future lies in our hands, to make or to mar, a time in which to pile up merits or to accumulate sins. It must be one or the other; we are to decide which it is going to be. And therefore the future is the land of hope, but not a mere vague hope. Rather is it a determined and confident hope, since it is based, not on our own abilities, but on God and His promises and graces. We know that if we ask Him, and if we do our own part, He will not give us a stone in place of bread; He will not turn us away from Him. "Him that cometh to Me, I will not cast out" (John 6:37). He who feeds the sparrows and clothes the lilies of the field will plenteously supply our needs, both material and spiritual; and moreover He will give us the grace to keep the record unspotted.

But striving to do this half the battle is to have our plan of campaign plotted out beforehand. As forewarned is forearmed, we should prepare ourselves to be ready for various snares and temptations, that so we may not be taken unawares and unprepared. For we shall in the future undoubtedly encounter many dangers to our souls, —temptations, trials, difficulties—and if we can fortify ourselves in advance against them, it will greatly help us. In this respect it is especially important to resolve to avoid all probable occasions of sin so far as is possible. If we always did this, we would be astonished by the fewness of our falls, for generally we slide into sin almost insensibly, and it happens because we have placed ourselves in what is called a probable occasion of sin, that is, in circumstances that are likely to cause us to fall. Therefore we will avoid such circumstances if we can. If duty forces us into them, then we will confidently invoke God's help since we are engaged in His work, and since we know that, as He has given us that work to do, He is bound to give us also the grace not to come to harm from it and, in fact, to profit by it. In this matter of avoiding occasions of sin we will be courageous and generous, so that if it be hard to give up someone or something that we know constitutes for us such an occasion, we will say: "God asks this of me, and I will not deny Him it."

That is the first thing in planning for the future (the avoidance of occasions of sin), and the second is to resolve to rise again at once after our falls, not to be unduly cast down in spirit: humbled, yes, but not in the least discouraged. In such circumstances, let us get to our feet, brush ourselves down (by confession), and say to God: "You see how feeble I am, Lord; take charge of me from now on." In this way our very falls will help us. And thirdly, let us be resolved to bear all trials gladly, remem-

bering their great value, that they are part of God's plan
for us, that they perform a most useful work in us, and
that they liken us to Christ and give us a share in His
sufferings, and therefore a share in the work of redemption, with the consequent share in His glory, as St. Paul
reminds us, saying: "If we suffer with Him, that we may
be also glorified with Him" (Rom. 8:17).

Fourthly, I would urge you to practice recollection:
keep your heart and mind in touch with God throughout
the day, and remember that He is always present and wit-
nesses everything. This recollection is of the utmost importance and is possible to all, even to the busiest of us.
It needs only a brief raising of the heart to God every now
and then, and a loving ejaculation; but it keeps us in tune
with Him. If we are not in tune with God, we cannot receive His messages in our heart, just as a radio receiver
will not pick up a message if it is wrongly tuned-in. A radio
set that is tuned to Denver will not pick up messages from
Chicago; and if our hearts are attuned to the world, or
even too much to our daily routine duties, they will not
pick up the voice of God. For that we need to be free from
distractions, to have purity of intention and a burning love
of God, and to remember that He is always present.

A final recommendation as regards the future: let us be
resolved to do always the holy will of God. Self-will being
the cause of all sin, it must be rooted out by stern and
courageous self-discipline. But God wills that we become
saints; in the Apostle's words, "This is the will of God, your
sanctification" (I Thess. 4:3). The carrying out of His will

is the sole road to sanctity, and therefore to happiness in both worlds; it is, in fact, the only safe path to follow and it infallibly leads us to God. His holy will, then, as shown to us by the prescriptions of the Rule of our Order or Institute, by the orders or wishes of our superior, and even by the happenings that befall us, must be our first and only consideration if we are wise. Indeed, since to this we have pledged ourselves by our religious vows, we have no choice in the matter. "Thy holy will be done": let that be ever in our hearts and on our lips.

There, then, are a number of resolutions for the future, and if we put them faithfully into practice we shall be able to profit fully by the graces and opportunities God continually and generously sends us. Like bees we will gather and preserve the honey from the flowers which God will put in our path. But we must remember that the flowers of God have this peculiarity: scent is not perceptible until the bloom has been plucked. Until then they seem more like thorn bushes; but the sharper the prickles, the sweeter and more precious is the flower. We should take full advantage of our thorn bushes, gather them, and, if the prickles draw blood, so much the better and the more profitable for us. May God, then, give us the grace to renew and observe our resolutions; may He be thanked and praised for having given us the grace and the courage to make them; and may we all water them daily by prayer for the divine help, that so they will blossom eternally in the garden of God's love.

XVII

SUFFERING

All through the ages mankind has been faced with the enigma and problem presented by suffering; this problem has even puzzled and disturbed many Christians. Why should an omnipotent and loving God leave us to endure agonies of suffering, mental or physical? How can we reconcile the sorrows and pains of the world with the goodness and kindness and wisdom of God? And thus the great question "Why?" rises on the lips of countless sufferers, and they are puzzled or resentful, or they even lose their faith in God. Mankind as a whole clings to the desire for happiness, it seeks to anticipate what it will have only in heaven, and therefore it fails to grasp the significance of human suffering. Because the world cannot appreciate or understand suffering, it cannot appreciate or understand Christ, who remains, as St. Paul said: "Christ crucified: unto the Jews a stumbling block, and unto the Gentiles foolishness" (I Cor. 1:23). Yet nothing manifests better than the Cross the wisdom and the power of God. Let us try again to see what we can make of this great problem.

First, by way of preparation for this task, let us try to have the purely spiritual outlook, to see things as far as

may be from the angle of God, that we may have some
prospect of piercing, so far as is permitted, behind the
cloud which conceals the motives and methods of God.
Although these are, of course, inscrutable in themselves,
we can, if we have a spiritual outlook, glimpse something
of them. For we know that there must be an adequate
reason and explanation of it all, that our difficulties in this
regard must be owing to our mental limitations, and that
therefore our distress at the thought or experience of
suffering is in reality groundless and illogical. "Out of evil
God bringeth good"; "to those who love God all things
cooperate to good"; and "God's ways are not our ways":
there we have three texts that go far to clear up the whole
problem and that in any event we should always carry in
our hearts. God is supreme wisdom, He is mercy and love
and justice; yet He allows or even sends suffering and
anguish. Therefore such things must be for a good purpose and must be productive of good. That is in essence
the outline of the position, and it remains but to fill it in.

The Cross, in some form or other, is inevitable for all of
us: that is the very law of our fallen nature. "Man, born of
a woman," says Holy Writ, "living for a short time, is filled
with many miseries" (Job 14:1). We all have our agony,
our scourging, our crown of thorns, our cross to bear. Born
through pain, in pain we die, and pain comes to us
throughout our lives from innumerable sources: from our
bodies, our hearts, our minds, our enemies, our friends,
from the devil, from our sins, and lastly from God. No
wonder the poet sings:

> To each his sufferings, all are men,
> Condemned alike to groan,
> The tender for another's pain,
> The unfeeling for his own.

That is an ever-present feature of life; and God meant that it should be so. Christ came to preach good tidings, especially to the poor and suffering, yet He did not come to take away poverty and suffering. On the contrary He said: "Blessed are the poor, blessed are they that mourn," and by His own passion He cast a halo around the world's sorrow, and won for all men strength to endure in peace. As someone has splendidly put it: "He came not to root up the thorns that sin had sown, but to teach our bleeding fingers how to wreathe them into a crown of glory," that is, how from our very sufferings to wring our eternal bliss. Thus St. Paul could write: "God forbid that I should glory save in the cross of our Lord Jesus Christ" (Gal. 6:14). All the saints have considered suffering a precious treasure, and, though we may not be able to welcome it for itself, we can and should welcome it for its beneficial consequences.

What are those benefits flowing from suffering, and why is it necessary that man should suffer? It is significant that the Latin *virtus*, for which we use our word "virtue," really means strength, endurance, manliness; and rightly so, for virtue cannot exist without these qualities. Our rebellious natures can be tamed only by painful effort, our self-love and self-will can be cured only by painful remedies. Pain, therefore, is the price that must be paid for health of soul.

Only through the crucifixion of self can we come to union with God, only the cross can strengthen and purify our character, and this it does if we use suffering aright. This God enables us to do, for He gives us the graces won for us on Calvary. Thus it is not in anger, but in love, that He sends the cross; His purpose is to heal our diseases, and draw our souls to His love in which alone is all happiness.

But suffering has another cause: it is the direct effect of sin, inevitable result of sin. Thus we bring it upon ourselves. The laws of God cannot be flouted with impunity; not only are sinners punished in the next world, but nearly always they are punished also in this life, either mentally or physically, and sometimes in both ways. At times this is so strikingly evident as to be frightening, so plainly does it show the avenging hand of God. "God is not mocked." Either through remorse and anxiety and unhappiness, or through actual physical disease, the sinner is stricken with suffering. Sin thus has to be paid for, and similarly the justice of God has to be appeased, which means that sin has to be expiated. This expiation is not necessarily exacted from the actual sinner, for all the human race (united in one body with Christ) is one in the eyes of God. Thus it often happens that He exacts and accepts expiation vicariously offered by another on behalf of the sinner. That is where the sufferings of a religious are of such value. "Without shedding of blood," says the Apostle, "there is no remission" (Heb. 9:22), and the debt remains after the sin has been forgiven. The wounds caused by sin have still to be healed, the baneful effects have to be removed; and by God's mercy suffering does this work, for, if it is rightly borne, it goes far to pay off the debt due to God's justice and also to heal the ravages of past sin. Thus does suffering that is borne penitentially gladden the heart at the thought of the crushing burden of debt that is wiped away.

And suffering has also the further value of detaching our hearts from creatures, and detachment is necessary if we are to be wholly God's and He is to be wholly ours. If we are attached to earthly things, God is crowded out of our hearts. Once again there is no room for Him in the inn. And nothing purifies the heart from worldly pleasures so rapidly and surely as suffering, if it is rightly considered and rightly borne. Caught in the prickly scrub of worldly pleasure, which instills poison into us, we have to be cured of it by having the thorns plucked out, a painful process. But it is most efficacious, and in this way God frees hearts from what would otherwise hold them in bondage. Suffering, indeed, can turn all things to gold. Thus, then, we are detached from earth's trifles, shown that we are but wayfarers on earth, and brought down to the bed-rock of reality, so that by it we are given a clarity of vision that can be acquired in no other way. Even as it is, we center our hearts too much on the passing things of the world. What, then, would we be like if our life were one of unalloyed happiness? We would seldom, if ever, think of God, and would become even more earth-bound than we are now.

I thank Thee, Lord, that all our joy is touched with pain,
That sorrows fall on brightest hours, that thorns remain—
That earth's bliss may be our guide, and not our chain.

Surely, too, we wish to share in the great work of the world's redemption, to take a part in the saving of souls. But this can be done only by means of the cross, and that cross must be the hallmark of all our work for them. A work is worthless and unable to promote the interests of God, however important or valuable it may be in the eyes of men, until it has been marked with the brand of the cross. That is why all notable religious undertakings have experienced great trials and tribulations. "In this sign [the cross] you shall conquer." By the cross, then, by our suffering, we can promote God's interests and help souls, and we can do that because Christ permits us and enables us to offer our sufferings on behalf of others in union with His own sufferings on the cross, and this because we are all one in Christ, all members of the mystical body of Christ; in other words, by reason of the fact of the communion of saints. In time of sickness, our pains and sufferings can powerfully help our fellow men, we can make vicarious atonement for them, after the example of Our Lord and in union with Him. This truth is a source of consolation when we are in pain, whether physical or mental. Indeed, it is when we are helplessly confined to bed and seem useless to everyone, that in reality we are of most use, both to the community and to the world at large; for it is then we are dearest to God, and our prayer is of most power. If God says "Bed" to you, bed is the only place where you can be of any use, for that is His will. Then can we say with St. Paul: I "fill up those things that are wanting of the sufferings of Christ" (Col. 1:24); that is, we supply that measure of suffering which Christ has left it to His members to supply. And thereby we fulfill God's intention.

In thus helping others by our pains we are at the same time winning our own spurs, for suffering is also a probation: it is God's way of proving us. All life is a probation, but we most truly and fully show what we are when we are suffering. And if the suffering or privation is voluntary, so much the more does it show our good will. "Self-denial," said Newman, "is the measure of love"; and the Book of Proverbs declares: "As silver is tried by fire, and gold in the furnace, so the Lord trieth the hearts" (Prov. 17:3). Therefore, if He tries us hard, it is all the greater favor, since it shows that He has great things in store for us for which He would have us qualify. Suffering is, then, a favor, and that is why, as we read in *The Wisdom of the Desert*, a certain hermit who was frequently sick and feeble wept and was sorely afflicted because for one whole year no sickness of any kind befell him. "Thou hast left me, O Lord," he cried, "and art unwilling to come to me this year." Indeed, nothing so likens us to Christ as patient bearing of the cross, which is the royal road to sanctity. The holy Curé of Ars said that if we flee from the cross we flee from Him who was nailed to it, and also that if we could go and pass a week in heaven we would know what a moment of suffering on earth was worth. Suffering, then, proves us and is of the utmost value to us; therefore God sends or permits it.

What virtues also it calls forth! What opportunities it gives! Opportunities of unselfishness, of kindliness, of patience, of endurance, of trust in God ("Even though He should slay me, yet shall I trust in Him"), and above all of charity. For suffering, accepted properly, can give us a quick sympathy for others, an understanding of their griefs and pains, a large-hearted and generous love. Teaching us also a prompter and more complete acquiescence in whatever may be God's will, it can promote us to a closer union with Him. It can also very efficaciously teach us humility, and will eradicate many of the vices or failings to which we are prone. All these fruits of suffering show that it can produce holiness in us. Yes, suffering can teach us many lessons that cannot otherwise be learned, or can otherwise be acquired only with the utmost difficulty. Perhaps you have heard the old English rhyme:

I walked a mile with Pleasure: she chatted all the way,
And left me none the wiser, for all she had to say.
I walked a mile with Sorrow: and ne'er a word said she!
But oh! the things I learned from her: when Sorrow walked
   with me.

Suffering is the great teacher. As no one is fit to rule others until he has himself learned to obey, so no one is fit to minister to others adequately and fully and understandingly until he has himself suffered. For suffering, that compassionate mistress, keeps a wonderful school, the school of God, in which wonderful things are taught. In that school of Christ we learn to carry out the twin commands: "Love ye one another" and "Bear ye one another's burdens"; and if we have learned those lessons of priceless worth, what else matters? Indeed, in view of the great benefits that flow from suffering, the wonder is that we have not heavier crosses to bear. But God knows our weakness, and He tempers our burdens to our needs and strength. The suffering He sends is not stern and forbidding, but kind and gentle, sweetened with love, the love of Him who sends it, and the love with which it is received. And through it all we hear crystal-clear the voice of the beloved Master: "I will see you again, and your heart shall rejoice. And your joy no man shall take from you" (John 16:22).

Happy, blessed suffering, then, of whatever kind it may be, or from whatever source it may spring! It is the gentle gift of God, the means of perfection. But this is so only if we take the spiritual view of our afflictions. To do this we must be careful to look beyond the mere human instrument of our sorrow or the natural event which causes it, and see the hand of God behind it. Otherwise there is great danger of reaping from it merely resentment or discontent or self-pity, and thereby throwing away or ruining God's gift completely. We have to remember that it is not the person or the thing that is primarily responsible for our suffering, but God. He asks us to accept it from Him, and He would hear us echo His own words: "The chalice which My Father hath given me, shall I not drink it?" (John 18:11.) He expects us to take up our cross and follow Him. It is all foreseen in the plan of our sanctification. Many centuries ago these wise words were uttered: "The perfection of man consists in suffering all things well, as if they happened to him of his own choice." Is it not true, as St. Francis de Sales points out, that not one of the mortals who are now immortal in heaven arrived there by any other way than that of continual trouble and affliction? And the same saint and doctor of the Church declares that "to suffer for God is to fill our hands with the purest and most precious of gold wherewith to purchase heaven. . . . The time of afflictions and contradictions is the beautiful harvest-time when the soul gathers in the richest benedictions of heaven. One day then is more profitable than six at another time." And, in fact, none of the pains and afflictions, sorrows and troubles of life, which we so dread, can really harm us. "To them that love God, all things work together unto good" (Rom. 8:28), wrote St. Paul to the Romans. It is only we who can harm ourselves, and we will grievously harm ourselves if we refuse to pick up the cross that Christ offers us. To bear the cross is the vocation to which His followers are called, and He walks before us bearing His own cross to encourage us.

> Stormy and sunless day:
> Wind-swept, rain-sodden road:
> Weary and long the way
> Under my heavy load.
> But ever before me I dimly scan
> The cross-bowed form of a Lonely Man,
> And through the sobbing raindrops falling

I hear His sweet persistent calling:
  "Child, I have need of thee.
Come, child, and follow Me."
  Fury of battle din,
    Battle of death and life:
  Raging forces of sin:
    Pitiless, endless strife.
But ever athwart the smoke-wreathed air
My Captain's banner is waving fair;
And through the roar of fray appalling
I hear His strong, persistent calling:
  "Child, I have need of thee.
Fight on, and follow Me."

  Follow Thee? Yea, my Guide,
    So Thou wilt lead me still.
  Let weal or woe betide,
    To Thee I yield my will.
But give me daily my cross to bear,
And a thorny crown for my brows to wear:
Then, when the shades of death are falling,
Oh, grant me grace to hear Thee calling:
  "Child, I have need of thee.
Come, child, to live with Me." [1]

Indeed He will richly reward us for our little spell of cross-bearing. And how He sympathizes with us! When He was on earth He suffered more by His sympathy for us than we actually suffer now. And even now does He not take on Himself the role of Simon the Cyrenean by helping us to bear the cross along the rugged road? Thus, if He strikes with one hand to heal us, He caresses with the other, so that in spite of all it is true, as He said: "My yoke is sweet, and My burden light" (Matt. 11:30).

[1] *Vocation*, by E. L. Thomas.

In view of all this, who would be so foolish as to dread suffering or to flee from it? Must we not, on the contrary, remember that love always involves suffering, even human love? A mother suffers for her child; a lover is glad to suffer for the loved one and so to help him or her. Love and suffering cannot be divorced. Hence, if we love Christ, we will long to suffer for Him and for those whom He loves. And that suffering will be experienced with gladness and received with love, for God wishes that we make our offering gladly, not grudgingly. "The Lord loveth a cheerful giver." We will therefore make our offering of suffering with joy; not with mournful, self-pitying resignation, but with love. Resignation is not good enough in this matter for those who are trying by their vows to be saints. It is not resignation that we must seek, but happy wholehearted acceptance, with thanks for the privilege of being allowed to suffer, and so to share Our Lord's cross.

Thus we see that the cross does not mean unhappiness. Happiness predominated (interiorly) in Christ's life on earth, and it is meant to predominate in ours: not external, worldly, transient happiness; but interior, spiritual, perpetual happiness. If the world is a vale of tears, it is also the garden of God in which He would have us be brave, strong, and joyous in the midst of toil and conflicts and disappointments. He rejoiced to suffer for His Father and for us, since His love was stronger than His pain; and He has won for us the same grace. Love solves the problem and makes the bitter sweet.

XVIII

CONFESSION

God in His love and mercy has not failed to give us whatever is necessary for our spiritual welfare or happiness. Having gone to the length of dying for us, He has also lavishly supplied us with supernatural helps, and notably with the graces that flow from the various sacraments. Each of these has a profound influence on our lives, strengthening, guiding, healing, each in its own particular way, and for each of these we owe a debt of gratitude. Not the least of these gifts is that sacrament which is the means appointed by God for giving us peace of mind and spiritual joy and for curing the wounds of the soul: the sacrament of penance, or, as it might well be called, the sacrament of peace. For by this sacrament countless sorrowful and grievously wounded souls, creeping to the feet of the Master, have been laved in the waters of   ment, have been washed clean, as the lepers
l and thereby healed in the Jordan, and have
᾽d that deep and lasting peace of mind for
᾽y were yet in sin, their tortured souls had
῏es, the sacrament of penance is a mar-
᾽nd an unfailing source of happiness

This being so, how sad and strange it is that many souls dread this sacrament! It seems incredible, yet such is the fact. Devised by God for our peace and happiness, it is used by the devil to frighten us, for he does all he can to keep us from this medicinal sacrament by warping our minds with unreasonable fears, unreasonable because such fears are groundless. When we consider calmly the purpose and the effects of this sacrament, we must surely love it, delight in it, and run to it as often as possible. What is there to dread in it? Nothing whatever. On the contrary, we have many reasons for cherishing it. God meant it to bring us comfort, and it does so; and if it has not this effect, that is the work of Satan, and we must therefore ignore his suggestions. Never shrink from this life-giving sacrament; never be so foolish as to fear it. But love it, thank God for it, and use it as often as you can because of the powerful effects it has on the soul, even though you may have no unforgiven sins to confess. More will be said about that in a moment.

But let us take things in order, and so start by considering what is necessary on our part if we are to receive this sacrament profitably. In addition to confessing our sins fully and plainly, we also need contrition (which includes a firm purpose of amendment) and, secondly, we have to make satisfaction, which means performing our penance. You know all that, but perhaps a few points in this connection may be made clearer for some of you; and in particular there are some mistaken ideas on the subject which are surprisingly common and which should be swept away, for they are often not made clear in instructions on this sacrament. We will come to these in due course.

But first, as regards contrition: perfect contrition (by which we mean sorrow because we have offended God whom we love) remits all mortal sin at once, even before we go to confession, provided that we have the wish and intention to confess such sin in the tribunal of penance. So, if ever you should be so unhappy as to fall into grave sin, remember that you are immediately freed from its guilt by an act of perfect contrition, without having to wait until you can make your confession.[1] This is because love of God and the state of sin cannot coexist in the soul. God has said in the Book of Proverbs: "I love them that love Me" (Prov. 8:17); therefore He loves you when you make an act of perfect contrition. But God, when He loves a soul, fills it with grace and thereby frees it from sin. If God dwells in a soul, that soul is in the state of grace, free from mortal sin. Moreover, if you love God you necessarily hate sin, and therefore your sin is forgiven. An act of perfect contrition is, as a matter of fact, the most perfect disposition we can have. Of course it must be accompanied by a desire and intention to confess, for we cannot be really contrite without having a wish for this sacrament, the more so because of God's command that we receive it, and also because of its effects.

Think of what the absolution in the confessional does. If we have only venial sins to confess, so that we are al-

[1] But, even so, confession is necessary in that case before receiving Holy Communion.

ready in the state of grace, it increases the amount of grace in us (all the sacraments confer grace), increasing our habitual grace, thus making us stronger and holier. It also gives us a claim to actual graces, that is, transient graces or helps in times of temptation or difficulty. It increases our security and peace, and lessens the temporal punishment still due for forgiven sin, that is, it shortens our purgatory. Moreover, it strengthens us against the danger of relapses into sin. Because of these effects, frequent confession is useful even though we may have only small venial sins to confess, or even though we have no sins at all to confess since our last confession; in that event it suffices to confess a sin of our past life, whether previously confessed or not, to obtain all these benefits.

And if, on the other hand, we should have a mortal sin to confess, then the absolution gives us habitual grace, filling us with sanctifying grace and restoring us to the state of grace. It also gives us a right to actual graces, as already explained; and it remits entirely the eternal punishment (hell) due to our grave sin, and lessens the temporal punishment (purgatory) also due to it. Also it probably causes a revival of all our previous merits which had been lost by our grave sin. Of course, good works done while in the state of mortal sin are devoid of merit.

Such, then, are the far-reaching and wonderful effects of receiving absolution in the sacrament of penance with the required dispositions. These required dispositions are that we should hate sin above all things, that we should have genuine sorrow for having sinned, and that we should have a firm purpose of amendment. I have just said that we must have genuine sorrow; but, when we actually go to confession, it is not necessary that we have perfect contrition (sorrow based on the motive of love of God), which some find it hard to have; it is sufficient to have imperfect contrition, which is technically called attrition, and which means having a lesser, though supernatural, motive for sorrow, such as the fear of hell or the harm that sin has done to our soul. Attrition is indeed useful and is a preparation for the reception of grace; hence Christ often spoke of the punishment awaiting the unrepentant sinner. He thereby gives us a fear of hell, a motive for attrition.

With our sorrow there is also our determination to make amends to God, so far as we can, for our past sins, that is, we are resolved to make satisfaction for them, and the nature of this satisfaction is fixed for us by the priest when he gives us our penance. The object is to compensate for the injury done to God, and also thereby to pay off, as it were, in whole or in part, the temporal punishment still due even after our forgiveness. And so Our Lord says to us in the Gospel: "Bring forth therefore fruits worthy of penance" (Luke 3:8). Indeed it is fitting that this liability to the pains of purgatory should thus remain after absolution, because we are thereby deterred from committing further sin, since to do so would be, among other things, to increase our purgatorial punishment; and also because it is in consonance with the justice and holiness of God, the first of which demands that we personally pay for our misdeeds, and the second of which necessitates our mortification before we enter His presence in heaven.

We now come to the various points, alluded to earlier in this chapter, about which there is often misunderstanding even among well-instructed Catholics, and which cause unnecessary anguish to souls. It is therefore especially important that these false ideas should be dispelled. The first concerns what is called the matter of this sacrament. The necessary matter (what must be confessed) is every mortal sin not previously confessed. We are bound to mention mortal sins from which we have not yet been absolved. Deliberately to omit these would be to annul the absolution and to add the sin of sacrilege. But only that is necessary. There is thus no obligation to mention any venial sins. To do so is optional, and they are forgiven whether we mention them or not, provided that we have the right dispositions (sorrow and a purpose of amendment). Venial sins, then, are called sufficient matter, which means that they are sufficient to make the giving of absolution possible if we have no mortal sins to confess. The reason why we need not mention venial sins is that all the venial sins of our whole life are remitted, whether mentioned or not, by means of the love and the sorrow that we have, and by the grace that is infused into us by this sacrament. Thus we need not make a long catalogue of venial sins; they need not be mentioned, so long as we have the right dispositions. If we have no mortal sin, the mention of one venial sin is enough to give something from

which the priest can absolve. This being so, you will see
that there is also no need to mention venial sins of long
ago.

I am stressing this because many think they must mention everything they wish to be forgiven; others suppose
that it is compulsory at each confession to mention a sin
of their past life, one that occurred previous to their
last confession. Such ideas are quite erroneous. All the
venial sins of our past life for which we are sorry are forgiven by every absolution, whether they have been mentioned or not. This fact also removes any cause for fear
about past confessions of venial sins. There we have no
need to rack our memory and to torture ourselves with
doubts about whether such and such a venial sin of our
past life was ever confessed. Only mortal sins have to be
mentioned. We should, therefore, not be scrupulous about
this. If we have nothing more than a few venial sins, or
only one, to confess since our last confession, we need not
mention any sins, venial or mortal, of our past life. Of
course, any unconfessed mortal sin must be confessed. In
the case of religious, it is better not to rake up mortal sins
that long since were washed away by God's mercy. Let us
not be scrupulous or superstitious, thinking we must mention the sins of our past life. They are all forgiven by every
absolution.

The second point on which there is often misunderstanding, and therefore unnecessary distress, is that there
may be some hidden forgotten mortal sin on our soul,

dating back perhaps to our youth, which has never been forgiven because it has never been confessed. Many persons have this haunting fear and are tortured by it. It is entirely groundless. Why? Because it is not possible for one mortal sin to be forgiven and others not to be forgiven. If we have several mortal sins on our soul, we are bound to confess them all; but if we should happen to forget some of them, they are all forgiven through the confession of the ones we remembered, although the obligation of confessing the others when we remember them at confession remains. For we are only bound to confess what, with reasonable care, we can remember. We are not bound to have an infallible memory. Let us remember those two truths. And the theological reason why the forgiveness of one such sin involves the forgiveness of all is that sin is removed only by the infusion of grace, which is brought about by the words of absolution. But any mortal sin excludes grace from the soul. Therefore if grace does come into the soul, as it does when we confess all the mortal sins we can remember, it follows that all sin must be driven out by it. Therefore one mortal sin cannot be forgiven without all of them being forgiven. You cannot be in the state of grace and have a mortal sin on your soul at the same time. Therefore, if you have done your best by confessing every hitherto unconfessed mortal sin which you could with reasonable care remember, you may be confident that any other mortal sin which you might later remember has already been forgiven by the absolution, though the obligation to confess it when next you remember it at confession remains.[2] If that fact were understood and realized, it would often bring peace to souls and dispel scruples; for it means that, as was said at the beginning of this paragraph, there is no need to worry lest there may be some mortal sin in the far distant past which we have forgotten to confess and which, we imagine, might therefore never have been forgiven. That is impossible, for the reason I have just given. Only if we deliberately omit to confess a mortal sin, does it remain unforgiven.

I have tried now to give you a clear idea of the effects of this sacrament, and also to remove some confusions and misunderstandings that sometimes occur on the subject. In conclusion, let me remind you of the elementary points that we should bear in mind in receiving this sacrament, more important than making a long and minute examination of conscience, since we need not mention any venial sins at all. 1. We must have genuine sorrow from a supernatural motive, either perfect contrition or else attrition. 2. We must have a firm purpose of amendment, a strong determination not to sin again, even though we may suspect from past experience that we probably will do those things again. The point is that, despite that feeling, we must have at the time of confession a determination not to do them. For unless we have that, our confession is obviously a mere mockery of God and worse than useless to our souls. Much better not to confess at all

---

[2] Hence every time you go to confession with the right dispositions all the sins of your whole life, up to that date, both mortal and venial, are forgiven, provided that you are not deliberately concealing a mortal sin.

than to retain a secret determination or will to repeat our sins. Notice that I refer to the will, for it is the will that matters; we may not be able to prevent our lower nature from being attracted to sin. Those, then, are the necessary dispositions, and God will always give them to us if we ask humbly and confidently.

By these means we will make good the harm we have done to ourselves by past sins: that is the merciful effect of this sacrament. But we have also by our sins wasted the grace which God has given us. We have to resolve to make better and more faithful use henceforth of the graces which God in His generosity sends us, and therefore "we should frequently beg God to enable us to repair before we die all our past losses of grace, and to reach that height of merit to which, in His first intention, He desired to lead us; which intention we have hitherto frustrated by our infidelities." [3]

By good use of this holy sacrament we will obtain the peace of God in our souls, and the joy of friendship with God is by its means always ours. What a great gift, then, is this healing sacrament which the good God has devised for us! Every time that we receive it we give glory thereby to God, and we appropriate to ourselves the merits of the passion and death of our Savior. Truly, then, the sacrament of penance, like all the others, is a sacrament of joy, for it delights, refreshes, and vivifies the soul. Never can we thank God sufficiently for it.

[3] Father Lallemant.

XIX

SPIRITUAL READING

The all-merciful God has given us many means of progressing along the road of perfection, but few are more efficacious than spiritual reading and prayer. Indeed, both St. Jerome and St. Augustine declare that these are the chief means of progressing, and in this two other doctors of the Church, St. Bernard and St. Francis de Sales, agree with them. It is evident that both these means are most powerful and can work wonders in us; and not only in those who earnestly seek after perfection, but also in those who are spiritually cold, hard, indifferent, and worldly. In its own degree this is as true of spiritual reading as it is of prayer, for we repeatedly hear of most unlikely souls who have been converted and whose whole way of living and outlook on life have been changed by the chance reading of a good book. Two such cases are known to everyone and will doubtless have already occurred to your minds: St. Augustine and St. Ignatius; two of the greatest saints whom the Church has produced and who have immensely influenced the faithful throughout the world. You remember the famous story of how St. Augustine, when still caught in the toils of a sinful life, heard one day a mysterious voice saying: *"Tolle, lege,"* ("Take and read"), and he accordingly picked up the book lying beside him belonging to his holy mother, St. Monica. In consequence his whole life was changed, and the notorious sinner and evil liver became a great saint and a doctor of the Church. So, too, was it with the holy founder of the Jesuits. When still a soldier, with no taste for spiritual matters, St. Ignatius, while confined to bed recuperating from a wound, chanced to pick up a book containing biographies of a number of the saints, and became enthralled with it. When at length he put it down, he was a changed man, and then began his new and wonderful life and work for God.

Spiritual reading, then, can have an immense effect, and even on the most unlikely type of reader. How much more so with us, who, despite our failings, are at least attuned to God, who already love God, who live only for His service, and in whose hearts the spark of divine love is burning and needs perhaps only the emotion and the considerations which are aroused in us by a spiritual book to burst into flame. Have we not found time and time again, and sometimes even when we did not feel in the mood for it, that a mere page from the right kind of spiritual book stirs us with love of God, with a desire to serve Him generously, with an impelling wish to be a saint and to emulate the heroic actions of those whose lives or whose exhortations we read? Deep calls to deep, even when in dryness or aridity our soul leaps to life in response to the holy advice and reasonings which we read, or the inspiring example of a saint's life which the book offers us. This we all know well by experience. Because it has this effect even on the unimaginative, spiritual reading is of such importance to us.

And then, too, what a peaceful, soothing influence this same reading has! We have perhaps been storm-tossed throughout the day, battling with difficulties, external or internal, worried, possibly discouraged; and then it comes to the time for our daily half-hour of spiritual reading. We pick up the book, perhaps even with some repugnance, and presently we find ourselves in a different world. Different thoughts, different standards, different ideals come before us and gradually possess us, little by little the cares of the day slip away from us, and an unction, a gladness, and a peace fill our hearts and souls and minds, so that when at last we put the book down we are reinvigorated and are filled with courage, with good resolutions, and with loving generosity toward God. That is one of the important functions which spiritual reading fulfills for us. Well, then, might Thomas à Kempis write in his *Doctrinale juvenum:* "Take thou a book into thy hands as Simon the Just took the Child Jesus into his arms to carry Him and to kiss Him. And when thou hast finished reading, close the book and give thanks for every word out of the mouth of God; because in the Lord's field thou hast found a hidden treasure."

And besides this beneficent effect, spiritual books store our minds with doctrine, with knowledge of God and His ways with the soul, in fact with theology. Evidently this knowledge is of great importance, for the more we know of God the greater help it is to our spiritual life, the less chance we have of going astray in spiritual matters, and the greater appreciation and realization of God we will have in heaven. If we store our minds with good things, with the riches of God, with a host of holy truths, we will grow in the knowledge and love of God. Many a religious, especially many a nun, would have been saved much anxious thought, much unnecessary scrupulosity, much misdirected effort, if she had only learned more about spiritual principles; and this she would have done in all probability if she had been more assiduous or more attentive in her spiritual reading.

But in this aspect of the matter there is one thing of which to beware; and perhaps a word of warning will not be out of place. We all know that when reading lives of the saints, and especially accounts of the austerities they practiced, we must be careful not to try too slavishly to copy them, for to do so would be beyond our power and the attempt would do more harm than good. For this reason one of the doctors of the Church has said that such things (extreme mortifications) are "for our admiration, not for our imitation." But the point is that the same caution and prudence must also be shown when we read spiritual books of a more general type, books, that is, which are not biographies, but which deal with the theory and principles of spiritual life. When reading such books, we need to be on our guard against applying to our own case everything that we read. Many persons, particularly those who are not very experienced or who have not discriminating minds, are apt so to apply what they read, and the result is not seldom most unfortunate.

We should note two things about such books. They are concerned with general principles, not with the application of those principles to individual souls. Each soul has its own difficulties and characteristics; what applies to one case may not be true of another. General statements have to be used with discrimination, and almost always they apply only partially to individual cases. Secondly, it is wise to remember that much that is in such books is not necessarily the official teaching of the Church, but only the private opinion of the author, even though the author may be a canonized saint, and even though the book bears an imprimatur, that is, the sanction of a bishop and an official censor. We sometimes hear people say that such and such an opinion must be correct because it is in a certain book, and that book has an imprimatur or has been approved by a bishop. Such people do not understand that this approval, or imprimatur, signifies only that nothing has been found in the volume contrary to Catholic doctrine and morals. But we are not to conclude that every statement in the book is vouched for by the Church, and therefore is to be accepted, and applied to our own particular case. Many of the statements we read in such books require qualification. They are too sweeping as they stand, and the author never meant them to be applied to every individual. In theological matters nearly every statement of a generalizing kind needs qualification. In other words, we must distinguish; that is, in certain cases and under

certain conditions, what the author says is correct, but not
so under all circumstances. Therefore we have to be prudent in this matter; otherwise some readers, especially the
scrupulous, are likely to become frightened and unhappy,
or puzzled and uneasy, and quite without cause, for they
are applying to their own case what really is not applicable to them at all. If in doubt on a point of this kind, it
is best to ask a priest, to whom you can explain the exact
circumstances. But if you ask him, be prepared to accept
his verdict. Do not consult a director if you are determined to adhere to your own view.

Apart from this danger, spiritual reading can always be
most helpful, and Father Augustine Baker declares that
"for spiritual profit this exercise may be esteemed next to
prayer." So we should cultivate a taste for it, if we have not
already such a taste; it can be cultivated and intensified.
If Montesquieu could say of ordinary secular reading that
"the love of reading enables a man to exchange the weari-
some hours of life, which come to everyone, for hours of
delight," much truer is this in the case of spiritual reading.
In this connection one can scarcely avoid special mention
of the wonderfully attractive writings of St. Francis de
Sales, that most human and gentle of the doctors of the
Church, who is at the same time one of the surest and most
easily understood of all spiritual writers. His sweetness
and his gentleness pervade every line he wrote, while his
sound common sense and his lucidity, coupled with his
love of God and of holiness, make him a joy to read. Many
great writers have extolled the merits of St. Francis as a

spiritual guide, but it is sufficient to recall the testimony of the great French preacher Bourdaloue, who declared: "After the Holy Scriptures there are no works that have better maintained piety among the faithful than the writings of this holy bishop."

Indeed spiritual writing such as his is truly a gift from God, showing us at what we should aim, showing us our own shortcomings in a vivid, yet not discouraging, manner, and imbuing us with a determination to amend them and to make strenuous yet peaceful efforts to advance in perfection. In fact, St. Gregory compares spiritual literature to a mirror which God puts before us, so that, seeing ourselves in it, we may correct what is amiss. And as a vain woman often goes to her looking glass to paint her lips, to rearrange her hair, or to titivate herself in a score of ways, so the Christian should have good books before him to show him his defects and the virtues at which he must aim, and to enable him to gain courage from the heroic examples of which he reads. St. Augustine uses another simile to stir us to love of spiritual reading. He describes good books as letters addressed to us by God and by the saints, which warn us of the dangers we must meet on our pilgrimage through life, point out where our enemies lie in ambush for us, tell us what virtues we shall need if we are not to perish by the wayside, encourage us to bear the labors and sufferings of the journey, and indicate to us the safe road to that happy country which the saints have already reached.

But it should be borne in mind that to study a spiritual

book is one thing, and to read it spiritually is quite another. Hence we must aim not merely at study which will give us a theoretical knowledge of truths, but at reading spiritually, that is, in such a way as will help us to gain a love for these truths and to put them into practice. In other words, we need to aim not merely at enlightening the mind, but at perfecting the will. Therefore St. Bernard admonishes us to try not so much to catch the meaning as the relish of what we read, and it is because they do not do this that some strange people actually find spiritual reading dry. In the midst of abundance they are dying of spiritual starvation.

Before beginning to read, we should ask God to enable us to profit by it, and we should read not from curiosity but from a desire to improve by our reading. For this we need grace, and God will give it to those who ask. Purity of intention, then, a firm resolution to put into practice what we read (so far as it is suitable for us), is what we need in our spiritual reading. Moreover, we should not read hastily, skimming over the words; for we need to give attention and to reflect on what we read, savoring the words, and even at times meditating on them if we would derive profit from them. The better the book, the greater the need for such treatment of it. Indeed a book like the *Imitation of Christ* cannot be read fast. If anyone attempts so to read it, he merely sees the words without in the least plumbing their depths. For this reason that book is particularly difficult to read; not that it is uninteresting or uninspiring, but precisely because it is so intensely moving and inspiring. One feels forced to stop after every sentence to meditate on it. And, in fact, that is the way to derive profit from spiritual reading. St. Ephraim says that one should turn back at times and read a particular passage two or three times over to extract its real flavor and meaning. There is, indeed, little advantage in reading much if we do not read well.

One last suggestion I would offer. An excellent practice is to keep a notebook in which to write down passages that have particularly impressed us in our reading. Thus after a little while we have a collection of all the best things we have read; as these items are in a compact form in one volume, reference can easily be made to them. Anyone who has tried this knows how useful and helpful it is. In this way we can retain the honey we have laboriously extracted and have it readily accessible at all times.

But above all be careful that for your reading you choose the right kind of book, the kind that will suit you individually and benefit you, for by no means will all spiritual books, no matter how eminent or holy their authors, do this. Some suit one type of soul, and others suit another, and "one man's meat is another man's poison." This difference is to be found in spiritual matters. We are surprised to note that some people persistently choose the wrong type of reading. They seem to have a facility for picking what will do them the least good, and may indeed do them positive harm. As in other matters, so in this let us be prudent. But at all events we should acquire (if we do not have it already) a love of spiritual reading, undertake it systematically, and not omit our daily reading on any excuse except that of sickness. It is one of our most precious spiritual exercises and duties, one that no one can afford to neglect.

XX

LIVING IN COMMUNITY

With rare exceptions the way of life sanctioned by the Church for those who would enter the state of perfection has always involved living in community. From time immemorial souls seeking God above all else have gravitated to religious houses. The very early Christians lived a common life, as shown in the *Acts of the Apostles;* in later times even the anchorites in the desert, to a large extent, clustered together and met in common to praise God in the Divine Office. In modern days so also do even those orders that most prize solitude, such as the Camaldulese hermits and the Carthusians, to name but two orders famous for their aloofness from the world. Numerous orders and congregations of monks and friars, and also the corresponding sisterhoods, have always lived in community and cherished this essential feature of their life. We can adduce many and good reasons for this: such as the dangers that arise from living alone, and the many virtues, such as self-restraint, unselfishness, mortification, and charity, which are exercised by living with others. But we need not dilate on those reasons now; the point is that community life is part and parcel of the life of perfection as lived under the religious vows, and therefore a most important factor for us and of crucial significance as regards our eternal prospects. How we react under the influences which are brought to bear on us by community life is the real test, perhaps the chief mark of our success or failure, and therefore we ought to consider closely this matter of living in community, its difficulties and its rewards.

We may say at the outset that those souls must be comparatively rare who find no difficulty, no mortification, in community life. Most of us have to live cooped up in one house with the same companions year in and year out, companions who probably have tastes, manners, and outlook in many ways differing from our own. Under these circumstances the life is likely to be irksome. Abbot Marmion [1] places it first among the mortifications inherent in the religious life, saying that, however much the common life is sweetened by fraternal charity, it none the less makes up a great part of our sufferings, for we inevitably jar on each other at times. He goes so far as to say that, even if religious houses were inhabited solely by saints worthy of canonization, they would still have to suffer from living in common. And to endure all that with patience and charity and without complaining is a real mortification and one that repeats itself every day. At first, perhaps, we do not notice it; moreover our pristine fervor helps us to ignore such difficulties. But as the years roll by, and as with increasing age our own ways become more fixed, and perhaps prolonged illness or nervous strain be-

[1] *Op. cit.*, chap. 9.

gins to tell on us, then a host of little things, absurdly trifling in themselves, begin to jar on us. When these are repeated day after day, year after year, at length they may assume exaggerated proportions in our minds and, unless we pull ourselves together and take serious steps in the matter, they may become almost intolerable. "Dripping water wears away a stone," and tiny annoyances daily repeated can distort our outlook and thereby ruin our spiritual life. Therefore we need to look into this matter carefully from time to time, and to see how we stand as regards it.

But do not imagine that it is a defect on our part if we find community life hard. It is largely a matter of temperament, and for that we are for the most part not responsible. In fact, even the saints have shared this feeling, and the great St. Bernard wrote: "My greatest mortification is community life"; [2] and when we reflect on the magnitude of his other mortifications, we realize the significance of his words. Nor indeed would we have it otherwise with us, for we surely desire and require all the mortifications we can get. If we found the life always easy and pleasant, well, in a sense it would be a blessing, but it would also be a loss; for the hardness of community life, besides being a valuable mortification and useful training, is also a fruitful means of providing us with never-failing opportunities for practicing many virtues. It is a school of virtues.

[2] Cf. St. Augustine: *"Sumus homines fragiles . . . qui faciunt invicem angustias."*

Consider especially how many chances it gives us of practicing the queen of virtues, charity, and how it trains us to charity. The hermit, the recluse, gets no chance of exercising his charity toward his fellow men (except in prayer for them): this is the chief drawback to that form of life and one of the main reasons for establishing the cenobitical life. Scores of times a day we have the chance and the duty of helping another (remembering that what we do for others we do for Christ), of refraining from unkindness in thought, word, or deed, in bearing patiently and lovingly with the defects of others, and thereby incidentally building up our own character. In this matter of bearing with others, let us note that a sense of humor is desirable. Often what might otherwise only annoy us has a comic side; and if we can see it, we will forget to be annoyed or peevish. "Laugh, and the world laughs with you": at any rate, cheerfulness will drive away much pettiness, selfishness, discouragement, and uncharitableness.

If community life thus gives abundant opportunities of practicing charity, it is the same with several other virtues, on which it is not necessary to dwell now. Run through them in your mind, and you will see that it is so: patience, obedience, modesty, humility, and so forth; they all flower in community life, and that life is designed to foster them. Therefore from the earliest ages of Christianity men and women desirous of serving God wholeheartedly and of following the counsels of perfection flocked into communities; and monastic lawmakers, notably St. Benedict, wrote strongly of the dangers of solitary life, and would not allow their religious to leave the community for a hermitage until they had passed many years in religion and had thus been trained and strengthened in the severe school of community life.

Difficulties do indeed exist in the religious life lived in community, but also solid advantages. To reap these advantages we have to strive hard against our own nature, and we have to follow certain guiding principles. Otherwise we only drift, and that is fatal. In brief, we must be imbued with the religious spirit, and see all the events of our daily life in a spiritual light and from the spiritual angle. By this means we will be profitable to our community, whereas otherwise we will probably be a drag on it, and a positive danger to it. The beautiful prayer of St. Francis of Assisi illustrates some of what we should aim at in this respect: "Lord, make me an instrument of Thy peace; where there is injury, let me sow pardon; where there is doubt, faith; where there is despair, hope; where there is darkness, light; and where there is sadness, joy. O divine Master, grant that I may not so much seek to be consoled as to console; to be understood as to understand; to be loved as to love; for it is in giving that we receive, it is in pardoning that we are pardoned, and it is in dying that we are born to eternal love." In a word, then, we must live for others and not for ourselves. A religious community has no room for a self-centered member.

A good community religious will be self-forgetful, and will always be eager to help the others, so that the motto of the house may well be, "One for all, and all for one."

Then harmony, peace, and happiness will abound, and then will be seen the truth of the Psalmist's words: "Behold how good and sweet it is for brethren to dwell in unity." Such a community is a jewel in God's sight, and such a happy state of affairs is the outcome, above all else, of charity, charity in thought and word and deed. Between a community that is steadfastly and uniformly charitable and one in which this virtue is not so prominently observed, there is all the difference in the world, and the difference can be seen in very many ways even by a casual visitor. A charitable community is a happy community and it is a holy community, for it has peace, without which those qualities cannot flourish. But peace can be obtained in a community only at the cost of sacrifices by each individual, because if each is seeking his own ends, his own will, and is not animated by a spirit of toleration and self-effacing humility, true religious life is impossible, and charity will soon vanish. Well does St. Benedict Joseph Labre say: "One should have three hearts: one, all of fire, for God; a heart of flesh for one's neighbor and tender above all for sinners; and a heart of bronze for oneself." And, by the way, if we have this, we will surely avoid that plague of the religious life: the formation of "particular friendships," so strongly condemned by spiritual writers. Indeed, such friendships do much harm, particularly because they injure charity. If two religious are inseparable friends, they soon become cut off by their own actions from the rest of the community, because no one else likes to break in on their conversation. And if others do the same, it means that the community becomes split up into groups or cliques. Such a condition is most pernicious for it is the end of real community life. No longer is such a community one united family. Furthermore, such exclusive friendships generally lead to uncharitable and harmful talk. Do your best, then, to be equally friendly with all, turn your back on none, and unduly favor none. That is the line followed by a good community religious.

This ideal is what we all aim at being: good community religious, for our spiritual progress to a surprising extent depends on that, and our duty to the community requires it. We are, then, bound to aim at that, and some of the means of reaching that goal, especially charity and the avoidance of particular friendships, have already been indicated. We mention here a few other helps, selected from a list of suggestions by the Ven. Augustine Baker, O.S.B., in his *Sancta Sophia*. These he offers in connection with another matter, but those about to be mentioned will also help us to be good community religious. Here, then, are some of his recommendations. To be wary and sparing in the use of the tongue. To avoid encumbering ourselves with business not pertaining to us ("Mind your own business"). To flee honors, offices, and the like. Not to crave this or that unnecessary thing, but to be content without what is superfluous. Not to question why such a thing was said or done,[3] but to hold patience and to let things be as they are. Not to complain of or accuse any. To abstain

---

[3] An important point, as a sure preservative of internal peace.

from appeals to superiors. To avoid the voluntary causing
or procuring of a change in our present employment or
place. To quiet and compose all manner of passions arising in the heart, and all troubles in the mind, and to preserve the soul in peace and cheerfulness. And in general,
simplicity in thoughts, words, and deeds.

Now it will readily be seen that all those admonitions
are conducive to peace within ourselves, and therefore
also to peace in the community as a whole. Consequently,
if we only follow that advice of the holy seventeenth-
century convent chaplain, we will indeed be good community religious and a boon to our companions. Thus a
community will remain a united family. The picture presented by such a united community has been impressively
drawn by Thomas à Kempis: "Against the wiles and ter-
rors of Satan a united community struggles and triumphs
. . . who toil in labors by day, give heed to sacred reading, instant in devout prayers . . . and put the demon to
flight. For they torment him mightily when they fast, they
tread him under foot when they beg pardon, they crush
him when they humble themselves; they terrify him when
they call upon Jesus, they torture him when they name
Mary, they drive him away when they sign themselves
with the cross, they conquer when they obey." Blessed,
then, is such a house, one which is united and at peace,
and such it can be only when each individual member
strives to be not only a good religious, but a good community religious, subordinating herself to the welfare of the
community, and for the sake of the community elimi-

nating all selfishness and other unpleasant traits or tend-
encies.

Is it not well worth while to strive for this end, whatever self-sacrifice and effort it involves? So long as you
put self first, with its pride, its self-seeking, and its self-
opinionatedness, you will not be happy, you will not be
holy, and you will be a thorn in the side of your fellow
religious, a hindrance to their advance in holiness. Strive,
then, in all things to subordinate self to the welfare of
others; think first of the community as a body, and self
last. Then you will be an instrument of peace, a bringer of
joy, a promoter of God's glory: things which you cannot
be if in any degree you put self before the community.

Finally let it be said that we will do this the more easily
and readily if we have before us a clear ideal of the religious life, a clear purpose in coming to it, a clear object
in living it. Such an ideal was years ago admirably expressed as follows: "I have left the world and the things
that are in the world in order that in the religious state
I may more fully learn and accomplish the will of God,
that I may live more secure from the dangers of temptation, and that, having at length completed the journey of
this life, I may merit to obtain with the faithful followers
of Christ the rewards of eternal beatitude. For I intend
henceforth to order my whole life to the service of God,
and to spend in religion the modicum of time that remains
to me. Wherefore I am ready to endure every labor, and
to obey the precepts of my elders, which they have framed

for my salvation and perfection, as becomes a novice, and as the religious state demands." [4]

There we have a beautiful and clearly expressed ideal and purpose, one which also admirably sums up the *raison d'être* of the religious life, and as such they form a fitting conclusion to these short conferences on the joys of that life. If every novice were made acquainted with that passage, and adopted it as his or her guide in the religious life, and remained faithful to it throughout "the modicum of time" that remains of this life on earth, then indeed would all our religious houses be still brighter jewels in the eyes of the Most High, and their members would taste to the full the joy of serving God.

[4] Thomas à Kempis, *Sermons to the Novices Regular.*

APPENDIX I

FOR THE CEREMONY OF A CLOTHING

This is a solemn and significant ceremony at which we are present today: that in which these souls present themselves to God to begin their novitiate, with the ultimate hope and intention of being His in this convent for the remainder of their lives. After many months of calm consideration and earnest prayer, they have deliberately turned their backs on the garish and deceitful pleasures of the world in order to seek that which alone is worth having: the service and the love of God. They have weighed the world in the balance and have found it wanting. Praised be God for having thus enlightened them! Truly this is "a spectacle for men and angels," one that must rejoice the courts of heaven. Gladly, then, we welcome these new recruits to the army of God. Ready and eager to fight for His cause, they say with the Psalmist: "I am ready and am not troubled" (Ps. 118:60).

And fight they will have to, for the whole of the religious life is a fight: a fight against the devil's operations in the world by a life of prayer and labor and mortification; a fight against the temptations besetting ourselves and others; and most of all a fight against ourselves, acquiring thereby self-discipline and self-conquest, since only thus can we be profitable servants of God. You, my dear sisters, know this well, and yet you come forward today to offer yourselves for this fight. May God grant you abundantly the necessary grace to persevere in that fight to the end, for the struggle is long and hard.

But all the necessary and valuable hardships of the religious life are sweetened and made delightful by the ever-abiding presence of God within us, by the knowledge of His love and approval, and by His habitual and actual graces lavishly bestowed on us. So it is that the Psalmist can say: "Taste and see that the Lord is sweet" (Ps. 33:9). Not till we have tasted can we realize how sweet He is, and this sweetness increases with the years of service, so that our Blessed Lord tells us: "My yoke is sweet and My burden light" (Matt. 11:30). It is made easy and delightful by the grace of God. Thus, then, does God fulfill the first half of His promise to all who leave kith and kin for His sake: "A hundredfold, and shall possess life everlasting" (Matt. 19:29). It is, indeed, a hundredfold reward, for we are given that real happiness in this mortal life which can come only from wholehearted service of God.

Wholehearted service: for half-and-half service brings misery to a religious. And what is the secret of giving wholehearted service? It is that we be meek and humble of heart, for if we are that, the other virtues will follow, since most sins come from pride and self-will. Therefore, when Christ wished to single out those of His qualities which we should particularly strive to emulate, He did not say: "Learn from Me to be heroic in mortification and endurance; learn of Me how to convert multitudes." No, He said something much more striking because of its contrast with what the world might expect from Him and from His soldiers. He said: "Learn of Me, because I am meek, and humble of heart" (Matt. 11:29). Set meekness before you, then, as the watchword of your religious life, meekness which implies obedience (for disobedience springs from pride), meekness before God and meekness toward your fellow men. "Blessed are the meek," said the Master, for meekness means a patient and loving bearing of the yoke, and Scripture tells us: "It is well for a man to have borne the yoke from his youth up." Happy, then, are you to have been called to this delightful yoke in the flower of your youth, and inestimable is the privilege thus bestowed on you.

A privilege indeed. It is not of your doing that you are here today. You have been called by God, who has whispered in the secret recesses of your heart, who has given you an attraction to the life of religion; in other words, it is He who has given you a vocation, and He has done this through His great love of you, even as He declares through the mouth of Jeremias: "I have loved thee with an everlasting love: therefore have I drawn thee, taking pity on thee" (Jer. 31:3). Never forget, then, what a great debt you owe to God for having chosen you out of so many millions to draw you to Himself as specially favored servants to serve Him in privileged intimacy.

But remember, too, that you will not yet be vowed to

His service. That is a future privilege which He holds in reserve to bestow if you show yourselves worthy during the novitiate. You have first to win your spurs. You must have a time of severe testing, and you must steel yourselves for it, being generously prepared to do and to endure all that God sends you during it through your superiors, and never forgetting that obedience is the only thing that can bring you safely through the novitiate, for it shows you invariably the will of God. If you keep His law, as shown to you by the Holy Rule and your superiors, He will do everything for you. "I will write it [God's law] in their heart," He said of the Israelites, "and I will be their God, and they shall be My people" (Jer. 31:33). So long as you never deviate from obedience, you have the assurance that you are doing God's will. Only time can tell whether that will is that you persevere to your profession, or that you return to the world. But whichever it is (and you will discover which it is by obedience), it is the best possible thing for you, for it is the most holy will of God. You have generously answered the call of God. Continue, then, to give yourselves to Him with complete generosity, holding nothing back, and He will continue to cherish you and to load you with blessings. That you may so act, and that He may consequently so reward you, is the earnest and humble prayer of all of us here today.

APPENDIX II

FOR A SOLEMN PROFESSION

My dear sisters, this is the greatest moment of your lives, and one that will have its effect for all eternity. All your life you will look back to this happy day, and will never cease to thank God for this tremendous privilege He has granted you of joining the select band of those who are vowed to Him. And throughout eternity, too, you will benefit by it since it will procure you a special place in heaven, a specially rich reward, so that in paradise you will be filled with the same thankfulness. Thus today is the most significant day in your whole life, for henceforth you are stamped with the seal of God and are His property.

For this day, of your own free will, unmoved by any considerations except your love of God and of souls, and your desire to save your own souls, you come to the altar to make this sacrifice of yourselves, which is the greatest offering you are able to make, and you make it in union with the supreme sacrifice of Christ on Calvary, the Most Holy Sacrifice of the Mass, since it is by virtue of that union that your offering is acceptable to God. And just as that sacrifice offered by Our Lord was a holocaust, that is, a complete offering in which nothing was held back, and

190

was, moreover, offered through love of God, so too this offering of yours this day will also be a holocaust, a complete giving of yourselves, and one that is inspired by your love of God. Henceforth you will be no longer your own, you will be and you ardently desire to be the chattels of God, absolutely at His disposal, to fulfill His wishes as made known to you through the commands of superiors. And because you do this of your own will, moved by grace, it is highly meritorious and pleasing to God, for this free offering of yourselves in union with Christ constitutes a supreme act of worship. You are separating yourselves from every created thing in order that you may be united to God alone.

The voice of God has sounded in your ears, and you have heard Him saying to you, as He said to Abraham: "Go forth . . . out of thy father's house, and come into the land which I shall show thee" (Gen. 12:1). Those words have come to you also, and your whole outlook on life has been changed by them. The finger of God has touched your hearts, and those hearts can henceforth be satisfied by nothing less than complete giving of yourselves to the divine Spouse. Therefore, leaving your homes, you have come to the place which God has shown you; and with the Psalmist you have said: "Here shall I dwell forever, for I have chosen this place." But at the same time recall Our Lord's words: "You have not chosen Me, but I have chosen you" (John 15:16); this act of yours is the result of the grace that has been freely given by God, the grace of vocation. He has called you and has given you the desire to obey His call. You have acted on that call and have corresponded to the grace given to you. May God be praised for it!

And the motive force behind this act of self-immolation on your part, what else can it be but love? It is only love of God, an overwhelming love, that can lead us to offer this great sacrifice, if we are to make it in the religious spirit. To cut oneself off entirely from earthly joys in order to give oneself completely to God is an act of perfect love. This is why God loads with immense blessings a soul that takes the vows and remains faithful to them, and grants to such a one unceasing joy. In fact, the taking of the vows is based on faith, hope, and charity (as you can easily see on reflection), and is a lofty act of each of those virtues. Hence God takes pleasure in receiving your vows.

Now you are of that band of whom St. John writes in the Apocalypse: "These are they who follow the Lamb whithersoever he goeth. These were purchased from among men, the first fruits to God and to the Lamb." Well does he say you were purchased; remember the words of St. Paul: "You are bought with a great price. Glorify and bear God in your bodies" (I Cor. 6:20). This dedication of yourselves has been made possible by the sacrifice of Christ on Calvary. You have been bought by His blood. See, then, that you never give Him cause to repent of His purchase; remember that you are His.

Not only has God thus made this act on your part possible, but He also, as I have just said, piles up blessings and joys on those who thus give themselves to Him. Be-

fore concluding I would draw your attention to three of
those rewards in particular. The first is that henceforth
all your actions, however indifferent or seemingly trivial
in themselves, have a special importance and value in the
eyes of God, because by reason of the vows they all share
in what is called the virtue of religion; that is, every little
thing you do becomes an act of worship, a religious act,
because it is done under the vows and through obedience.
And similarly an act that is itself meritorious, such as an
act of mortification or of charity, henceforth acquires an
added value because of the vows. In consequence, all that
you do from now on will be especially pleasing to God
and an act of worship offered to Him.

The second great benefit resulting from the vows is that
your soul becomes so pleasing to God that today He remits
entirely (according to a well-founded theological opinion) any debt of temporal punishment still owing for past
sins, so that your soul is completely cleansed, just as when
one receives baptism, and it is as if you had received a
plenary indulgence. Theologians are to a great extent
agreed in teaching this. Thus you start again with a clean
slate today; you are given a second chance to keep your
record unspotted. What a great cause for joy this is, and
how fortunate you are!

The third blessing and cause for joy is that henceforth
your profession will be an unfailing source of happiness
to you; because on account of it God Himself undertakes
to reward you richly, and He will not be unfaithful to His
promise. With happy generosity you have given Him

everything, and He in return will yet more generously fill you with joy. For He is the source of all happiness, and to you He promises what He declared to Abraham: "Fear not, Abram, I am thy protector, and thy reward exceeding great" (Gen. 15:1). There you have it. He is henceforth your reward exceeding great. And this reward will be experienced both in this life, by reason of your knowledge that you are at all times greatly pleasing God, the knowledge therefore of a good conscience (which is the only basis of real happiness), and yet more will it be experienced in the next life, for you are laying up rich spoils for eternity and thereby fulfilling Our Lord's exhortation: "Lay up to yourselves treasures in heaven, where neither the rust nor moth doth consume, and where thieves do not break through nor steal" (Matt. 6:20).

These three great blessings and rewards the all-loving God heaps upon you this happy day. Let your hearts dilate in thankfulness; show your deep gratitude throughout the remainder of your lives by your most faithful service of such a loving Master. My final word to you is that of St. Paul to the Philippians: "Rejoice in the Lord always; again I say, rejoice. Let your modesty be known to all men. . . . Be nothing solicitous; but in everything, by prayer and supplication, with thanksgiving, let your petitions be made known to God. And the peace of God, which surpasseth all understanding, keep your hearts and minds in Jesus Christ" (Phil. 4:4–7).

248
H   581
Hemphill
    The joy of
serving God

S. M. Pherse 3/16/7

248   581
H
Hemphill
    The joy of
serving God